60 Days of Purpose

A DEVOTIONAL JOURNAL
TO DEFINE YOUR DESTINY
& ACHIEVE TRUE SUCCESS

Karen Conrad

Harrison House

Shippensburg, PA

T0022445

Published by Harrison House Publishers
Shippensburg, PA 17257

ISBN 13 TP: 978-1-6803-1942-2

ISBN 13 eBook: 978-1-6803-1943-9

For Worldwide Distribution, Printed in the U.S.A.

1 2 3 4 5 6 7 8 / 26 25 24 23 22

Dedicated to my amazing husband,
Dave. I love you and our wonderful
life together. You're the best, baby!

Contents

Introduction

This devotional is based on my book, *The Promise of Purpose,* and is a compilation of the beautiful truths the Lord has made real in my life since the day I discovered He has a purpose for me. God was working in and through me even before I understood His heart and intention about purpose, and He was preparing me for what was ahead in my life. I am excited to help you discover your God-given purpose and vision and lead you on a path to making it a reality.

My prayer as you experience this devotional is that God will reveal how He lovingly and intentionally created you for a purpose and what that purpose is. There are encouraging tools, as well as practical methods and applications within its pages. I also share processes the Lord has given me to combat fear and limitations.

Each day has an Activations section to help you process the information on a more personal level and apply it to your life. There is also a daily Declaration to help feed and fuel your faith. You are in for an exciting journey that will change everything you ever thought about yourself! I pray you will find your unique place as you begin to understand His purpose for your life.

You Are God's Unique Creation

You saw me before I was born. Every day of my life was
recorded in your book. Every moment was laid out before
a single day had passed. How precious are your thoughts
about me, O God. They cannot be numbered! I can't even
count them; they outnumber the grains of sand! And when
I wake up, you are still with me! (Psalm 139:16-18, NLT)

Purpose is God's display to the world of His workmanship in you. God has uniquely and lovingly created you, and your purpose is a result of God's intentional design and plan. God thought about you and wrote the intimate details of your formation in His book. He then formed you according to His plan while you were in your mother's womb. God was present at your birth, and your days were actively shaped.

This passage in Psalm 139 talks about grains of sand and God's precious thoughts about each of us. I love the beach for its beauty and inspiration and joy. When walking on the beach, I glance down at the sand and am overwhelmed to realize that God's thoughts of me outnumber every single grain. It can be almost beyond my ability to comprehend.

God created you in His likeness to have an intimate relationship with you. He purposed that your life would be full of creativity and achievements in the context of love, peace, health, and prosperity. Jesus created you for good works. When you were born again, you became a new creation, transformed by Jesus. You now have specific divine attributes, rights, and opportunities. Your priority is a relationship with God, and what you do in life flows from that. God purposely designed you, and out of that heavenly design, He planned and prepared your life for achievement. He has positioned you to succeed in your purpose with His loving help.

Declaration

I am beautifully and wonderfully made. I have been created in the likeness of God for a personal, intimate relationship with Him and designed for a unique purpose. God has positioned me for success.

Activation

Think about God being present at your birth. He welcomed you into the world and celebrated your life. How does that make you feel?

Journal your thoughts about how God has seen every moment of your life through the eyes of love, acceptance, compassion, and grace.

_____

_____

_____

_____

_____

_____

_____

_____

_____

_____

_____

_____

_____

_____

_____

You Have a Distinctive Purpose

Then the Lord said to Moses, "Look, I have specifically chosen Bezalel son of Uri, grandson of Hur, of the tribe of Judah. I have filled him with the Spirit of God, giving him great wisdom, ability, and expertise in all kinds of crafts. He is a master craftsman, expert in working with gold, silver, and bronze. He is skilled in engraving and mounting gemstones and in carving wood. He is a master at every craft!" (Exodus 31:1-5, NLT)

A great example of being purposely designed and called can be found in Exodus. God anointed Bezalel as a skilled craftsman with a purpose. Moses received the instructions to build the Tabernacle, but God gave Bezalel the purpose—the creative empowerment to do and accomplish the work. That is incredible. God had already placed the gifts of creativity and beauty into Bezalel. Throughout his life he trained, practiced, and became a master craftsman. When the Lord filled him with the Spirit of God, Bezalel was fully equipped and had an uncommon advantage for his purpose. Walking in your purpose is part of God's good works He has prepared for you.

God has prearranged a good life for you. He has not planned a disastrous life, but an abundant life. He has provided everything you need to live the life He has made ready for you. He thinks very highly of you; He sees great things in you; and He gave you gifts because He trusts you. God has so much He wants to do through you. He loves you and has a beautiful life designed specifically for you. He wants you to enjoy your time on earth and participate in having His Kingdom come and His will be done in your life.

Declaration

The Lord has placed in me the gifts and talents to fulfill the purpose He designed for me. I am fully equipped to step into my destiny.

Activation

What are some things you have been fascinated by since you were a child?

Journal about a time you felt your gifts were being fully utilized. (This may not be something related to your current job or career.)

_____

_____

_____

_____

_____

_____

_____

_____

_____

_____

_____

_____

_____

_____

_____

_____

_____

God Calls You a Coworker

For we are God's fellow workers; you are God's field, you are
God's building. According to the grace of God which was given
to me, as a wise master builder I have laid the foundation, and
another builds on it. But let each one take heed how he builds
on it. For no other foundation can anyone lay than that which
is laid, which is Jesus Christ (1 Corinthians 3:9-11, NKJV).

Y ou are God's garden and God's building. He has
given you the grace, the supernatural power of
transformation, to do what He has called you to
do. A grace that is a special endowment for your task or
purpose. Grace is God's ability, strength, and power at
work in you. God gives you favor that enables you to do
and be everything He says you can do and be. God's grace
comes to you unmerited. He has already done everything
by grace for you, and you have already received it into your
born-again spirit. He has given you every spiritual blessing
(Ephesians 1:3), and belief and trust (faith) is your reac-
tion to Him. By faith, you reach into the spirit realm and
receive what God has already given you.

In these verses from 1 Corinthians 3, Paul said there is
no foundation other than Jesus Christ. God laid the foundation, which is Christ, and He completes the foundational

work in you. And before the foundation of the world, He equipped you for your purpose. He partners with you for success. The activities of your life are a form of worship to bring attention to God's greatness and His goodness. Paul describes this as well in Colossians 3:23 (TPT), when he wrote, *"Put your heart and soul into every activity you do, as though you are doing it for the Lord himself and not merely for others."*

Declaration

I am God's coworker, garden, and dwelling. I will stand on the foundation of Jesus Christ and allow the Master Builder to do His work in me.

Activation

The description in Day 3's opening verse regarding your relationship with God is astounding. You are a coworker with Him; you are His garden and His dwelling place. Do you think of yourself and God in these terms? Why or why not?

Write what you think God sees when He looks at you. Then ask Him to tell you what He sees when He looks at you.

DAY 4

You Have Been Given Diverse and Varied Gifts

Every believer has received grace gifts, so use them to
serve one another as faithful stewards of the many-
colored tapestry of God's grace (1 Peter 4:10, TPT).

A re you under the impression that you don't have
gifts or talents? Do you feel that God hasn't given
you what you need to succeed? Those are lies. You
can get that out of your thinking completely and hold on
to this beautiful verse in 1 Peter 4:10. A *grace gift* in the
Amplified Version of the Bible is defined as *"a spiritual talent, an ability graciously given by God."* You can be assured
that He has given to you, and you have received a special
gift, a spiritual talent, an ability graciously given by God.
Use it!

Sometimes you may feel as though you want to be like
other people. Be aware that it's a terrible waste of time and
energy to compare yourself with others. God gave your
gifts to you and their gifts to them. This verse, also in the
Amplified Version of the Bible, says that God has given us
"diverse, varied gifts and abilities." You must stop looking at
what other people are doing and instead seek God for what

you've been called to do. Coveting someone else's gifts and talents won't help you discover your own. Once you seek Him and learn what you're called to do, a grace reservoir of gifts and talents will be revealed.

Declaration

I have a reservoir of gifts and talents designed specifically for me. I believe God has designed and fully equipped me for my purpose.

Activation

What spiritual talents do you believe you've been given? Are you currently using them?

In your journal, list the special gifts and talents you believe are yours. Ask a trusted friend what gifts he or she sees in you and compare.

_____

_____

_____

_____

_____

_____

_____

_____

_____

_____

_____

_____

_____

_____

_____

DAY 5

The Father of Lights Gives You Good Gifts

Every good gift and every perfect gift is from above, and
comes down from the Father of lights, with whom there is
no variation or shadow of turning (James 1:17, NKJV).

T he gifts and talents God has given you are perfectly
designed for you. You can relax, knowing He values
what He has given to you and that you are complete
in Him (Colossians 2:10, NKJV). I am so encouraged by
this verse in James 1. The gifts He has put in me are good,
perfect, and from Him, the Father of lights! There is no
reason to fear being overlooked or undervalued. He wants
to see those gifts and talents used for His Kingdom and
acknowledged with value even more than you do. And He
will bring the increase: *"I planted, Apollos watered, but God
gave the increase. So then neither he who plants is anything,
nor he who waters, but God who gives the increase"* (1 Corinthians 3:6-7, NKJV).

Do you wonder sometimes what the Lord thinks about
you or how He sees you? God says that you are where you
are on purpose, not by accident. And if you are in a bad
or difficult place because of your own decisions, don't

lose heart. God can and will help you. He has appointed, placed, and purposefully planted you so your fruit will remain and be lasting.

As you understand and function in the gifts and talents God has given you, success comes supernaturally through Him. Your success is imminent when you're pursuing God in His purpose for your life. Isn't it amazing that God thinks you are a worthy bearer of His glory and wonder?

Declaration

The Father of lights has given perfect gifts to me. My Father promises He will prosper me. I will walk into today, knowing my success is imminent.

Activation

When you think about the majesty of God, how do you feel about discovering the gifts He designed specifically for you?

God equipped you with gifts, and He promises to bring the increase. Take time to think about that, then journal your thoughts and prayers.

_____

_____

_____

_____

_____

_____

_____

_____

_____

_____

_____

_____

_____

_____

Your Determined Purpose Is to Know God

I want to know Christ and experience the mighty power that
raised him from the dead. I want to suffer with him, sharing
in his death, so that one way or another I will experience the
resurrection from the dead! (Philippians 3:10-11, NLT)

Paul said his determined purpose was to *know God*.
The word "know" in the Greek means "to experience." That rocked my world. Paul recognized that
his determined purpose in life was to experience God personally and intimately, which is the foundational purpose
in all our lives. With that as a foundation, Paul went on to
accomplish amazing things through his own unique purpose—he knew how to keep first things first.

The starting point for understanding the purpose for
your life is to have a heart-to-heart connection and relationship with God. In that relationship, you will learn to
understand the real you, based on who you are in Jesus.
Your particular purpose is revealed in your personal relationship with God. Everything springboards from there.

How do you develop this kind of relationship? I had
been taught to spend time in my "prayer closet," which, to

be candid, did not sound very appealing to me. As I began to spend quality time (not in the closet), praying, studying the Word, and talking with God as if He was sitting on the couch with me, I quickly discovered He wasn't anything like I thought. After I let go of old religious ideas and became aware that He is in me and with me, I felt as though I had a new best Friend!

Declaration

I want to experience Christ and the power that raised Him from the dead. I will make my personal time with the Lord a priority. I will purposely develop a heart-to-heart connection with the Lord.

Activation

What does your time with the Lord look and feel like? Do you dread it or look forward to it? Do you need a change of perspective?

Journal some thoughts on how to change your perspective. Then ask the Lord what He would like to do during your time together.

_____

_____

_____

_____

_____

_____

_____

_____

_____

_____

_____

_____

_____

_____

_____

Purpose Flows from a Heart-to-Heart Relationship with God

And this is eternal life, that they may know You, the only
true God, and Jesus Christ whom You have sent. I have
glorified You on the earth. I have finished the work which
You have given Me to do (John 17:3-4, NKJV).

Jesus demonstrated a heart-to-heart relationship
with the Father while He was on earth. He was pres-
ence-driven and purpose-shaped. Your priority is to
have an intimate relationship with God, and out of that
comes your life's accomplishments. Jesus revealed this in
the Scripture in John 17:3-4, which is a conversation He
had with His Father a short time before Roman soldiers
arrested Him and took Him into custody.

A bit of translation from the Greek language provides
further understanding. The word "life" in this passage is *zoe*,
and it means "the quality of life that is possessed by the one
who gives it." Jesus is offering to everyone the same quality
of life He enjoys with the heavenly Father, which includes
the same love, closeness, acceptance, anointing, authority,
and so forth. Jesus referenced this same word, "life" *(zoe)*,

earlier in John 10:10 (NKJV): *"I have come that they may have life, and that they may have it more abundantly."*

To experience God is to experience His character; and we learn much about His character through Jesus: the suffering Messiah, the children's Champion, the Leader, and the Teller of stories. These and so much more are hints of God's character and help in our ability to know Him.

Declaration

Experiencing the God of the universe is totally possible for me. I have the same quality of life that Jesus had. I am going to walk in it!

Activation

What are some attributes you associate with God? What are some attributes you associate with Jesus? Are they interchangeable in your mind?

Journal some different ways you can begin to know God better. Look for verses that specifically speak about God's character.

_____

_____

_____

_____

_____

_____

_____

_____

_____

_____

_____

_____

_____

_____

Faith Works in a Love Environment

And this hope is not a disappointing fantasy, because we can now experience the endless love of God cascading into our hearts through the Holy Spirit who lives in us! (Romans 5:5, TPT)

H ope is an anchor to our soul (Hebrews 6:19), and God does not disappoint. God is love, which is the strongest attribute of God's character. He so loved the world that He gave His only Son, Jesus (John 3:16). *Love* means to value, hold in high regard, cherish, and consider precious. God has designed you to feel and experience His transformative love for you in your heart! Your heart is the seat of your value, self-worth, and identity.

When you experience His love, it impacts your trust in God because, in a love environment, faith works. A benefit of experiencing God's love is being able to love others. God's love teaches you how to treat others in a manner key to your ability to walk out your purpose. Purpose is a proportionate mixture of what you do and how you do it. Purpose demonstrated in the context of character and love produces a reputation that Proverbs 22:1 describes as better than *"great riches."*

You can receive love from God freely and without limitation, and it's not something you need to manufacture. Romans 5:5 says that God's love is poured into our heart by the Holy Spirit. And Jesus said that love is the number one way His followers will be recognized. The Bible's "Love Chapter" (1 Corinthians 13) tells us that without love, everything else is meaningless. But with love, nothing is impossible.

Declaration

I have the endless love of God cascading into my heart through the Holy Spirit. I will experience all that the love of God has for me.

Activation

Think about the love of God and how you experience it every day. Ask the Holy Spirit to bring God's love to your awareness.

Journal your thoughts about God's infinite love and contrast them with thoughts about your finite love.

_____

_____

_____

_____

_____

_____

_____

_____

_____

_____

_____

_____

_____

_____

_____

_____

There Is a Heavenly Blueprint for Your Life

Everyone who comes to me and hears my words and does them, I will show you what he is like: he is like a man building a house, who dug deep and laid the foundation on the rock. And when a flood arose, the stream broke against that house and could not shake it, because it had been well built. But the one who hears and does not do them is like a man who built a house on the ground without a foundation. When the stream broke against it, immediately it fell, and the ruin of that house was great (Luke 6:47-49, ESV).

There is a heavenly blueprint for your life; and in your experience with Jesus, you can hear His words and understand what your purpose is and how to walk it out. In life, you may experience overwhelming circumstances, forcefully attempting to bring destruction to your life and purpose; but according to God's Word, you cannot be shaken. No matter what floods come against your life, you will not be destroyed. Your life is well built and structured upon God's strength—not your own works.

Those who experience God but don't act upon His words subject themselves to a life susceptible to disappointment and even destruction. In all our ways we want to acknowledge Him and allow Him to build our house and direct our paths (Proverbs 3:5-6).

You operate out of a relationship with God, and your life, activities, and work are reflections of Him. He calls you His workmanship, His garden, His field, and His fellow worker—He promises to bring you increase, life, health, and protection. You bring Him glory in the way you conduct yourself and by accomplishing what He gives you to do. Actively experiencing God and being shaped by Him are keys to being able to withstand turbulence in your life. The key to a solid house is the rock that it's built upon—the true solid rock of Jesus Christ.

Declaration

By the grace of God, I have built my house on the firm foundation of Jesus Christ. No matter what comes, I will not be shaken.

Activation

How would you describe your foundation? Is your life built on Jesus Christ, the only true Foundation, or something else?

If you were to imagine a blueprint for your life, what would it look like? Write some highlights of this blueprint, and then ask the Lord to add to them.

_____

_____

_____

_____

_____

_____

_____

_____

_____

_____

_____

_____

_____

_____

_____

_____

DAY 10

Get Ready to Dream Big with God

and have put on the new [spiritual] self who is being continually
renewed in true knowledge in the image of Him who created the
new self—a renewal in which there is no [distinction between]
Greek and Jew, circumcised and uncircumcised, [nor between
nations whether] barbarian or Scythian, [nor in status whether]
slave or free, but Christ is all, and in all [so believers are equal
in Christ, without distinction] (Colossians 3:10-11, AMP).

Years ago, I had based my self-worth and identity on a foundation of being liked and accepted. When you do that, fear, failure, and rejection are around every corner. At that time, I didn't have a solid foundation in Christ Jesus, or my identity founded in Him. Really, my identity was built on shifting sand. I look back now, realizing I was so full of fear and anxiety, it probably came through loud and clear in every interaction I had. Unlocking your purpose through an intimate relationship with the Lord will establish your identity in Him, and much of your daily anxiety will be replaced with confidence.

Let me reassure you: We all have a unique purpose, designed by God. I want you to discover and develop that God-given purpose to achieve your full potential. I want to see purpose change your life as dramatically as it has changed mine. Your relationship with God is a love journey—a lifetime of discovery—where you come to know who He is, who you are, and how to accomplish what He wants you to achieve. I promise you, His plan for your life is better than anything you could imagine on your own, so get prepared to dream big with God.

Declaration

God has created me new in His image. God's plan for my life is better than my plan. I am going to dream BIG!

Activation

How do you feel about your identity? On what do you base your acceptance, acknowledgment, and confidence?

Journal some of your self-talk during the day. Compare it to how you feel about your identity. Are you talking to yourself as someone who is *equal in Christ, without distinction*?

_____

_____

_____

_____

_____

_____

_____

_____

_____

_____

_____

_____

_____

_____

_____

Operating in Your Purpose Brings Favor

> Then Mordecai told them to reply to Esther, "Do not think to
> yourself that in the king's palace you will escape any more than
> all the other Jews. For if you keep silent at this time, relief and
> deliverance will rise for the Jews from another place, but you
> and your father's house will perish. And who knows whether you
> have not come to the kingdom for such a time as this?" Then
> Esther told them to reply to Mordecai, "Go, gather all the Jews
> to be found in Susa, and hold a fast on my behalf, and do not
> eat or drink for three days, night or day. I and my young women
> will also fast as you do. Then I will go to the king, though it is
> against the law, and if I perish, I perish" (Esther 4:13-16, ESV).

Esther is my favorite example of someone who discovered and lived out her purpose. The book of Esther reveals how God prepared Esther for a special purpose and orchestrated the intricate events and details of her life. Esther's mother and father had passed away, and she lived with her uncle, Mordecai, as a young, single woman. God knew her purpose was to become queen of the empire and rescuer of the Jews, but Esther wasn't born with that knowledge. Throughout the story, you can see how God kept His hand of direction on her, working on her behalf. (I encourage you to read the entire book.)

Operating in your purpose—in alignment with God's design—brings favor. Esther experienced God's favor during a difficult situation that required risking her life to speak out on behalf of her people. What a heavy load for a young girl to bear! Esther was in the palace, facing a huge challenge. She had to determine if she was willing to potentially give her life for her people. Was it the right thing for her to do? What was the plan and the timing? Purpose is often revealed in an idea of what to do (vision), and then other factors come into play, such as methodology (how), timing (when), and collaboration with others. All these things worked together in Esther's purpose to bring success and deliverance for the Jews.

Declaration

I will put my past behind me and walk into a victorious future. I was born for such a time as this.

Activation

In Esther's young life, she had much that could have limited her success. She was orphaned, kidnapped, forced to become a concubine, and more. How do you think it was possible for her to thrive?

Journal some thoughts about breaking through hardship to experience victory in your life.

_____

_____

_____

_____

_____

_____

_____

_____

_____

_____

_____

_____

_____

_____

_____

DAY 12

Trust in the Lord Develops Confidence

Trust in the Lord with all your heart, and do not lean on your
own understanding. In all your ways acknowledge him, and
he will make straight your paths (Proverbs 3:5-6, ESV).

You can face challenges as a victorious overcomer
rather than a victim when your confidence is in
God, His consistency, His love, and His generosity toward you. His plans are for your good and not for
destruction—to bring you hope (Jeremiah 29:11). The
deeper your relationship goes with God, the greater your
trust in Him grows, knowing He'll provide for you in every
situation. You are building a personal history with God
based upon trust in who He is and what He has already
promised to do.

Esther is an inspiring example of someone willing to
be used by God to bring about His desired outcome. She
received His favor and ability to accomplish her divine
task (her purpose). She was then granted a larger role in
leading the kingdom than she could have attained on her
own. Her willingness was a key factor in stepping into her
purpose, as was her confidence that God would do what
He said He would do.

You are designed in the image of God, and He specifically created you with a free will. He has a plan and a purpose for your life. However, your free will and your choice to participate are active ingredients to your success. You must step out and choose.

Declaration

I will trust in the Lord with all my heart. I will not be a victim in my life. I am willing to be used by God.

Activation

Describe your trust level with the Lord.

Make a list of the times you were able to fully trust the Lord. Make another list of the times you were not able to believe He would do what He said. Ask the Lord to give you insight into both lists.

_____

_____

_____

_____

_____

_____

_____

_____

_____

_____

_____

_____

_____

_____

DAY 13

Jesus Perfectly Lived Out His Purpose

> The thief does not come except to steal, and to kill, and to destroy. I have come that they may have life, and that they may have it more abundantly (John 10:10, NKJV).

> ...For this purpose, the Son of God was manifested, that He might destroy the works of the devil (1 John 3:8, NKJV).

Jesus is the perfect Model of someone who lived out His purpose. Though His purpose was divine, we can learn much from Him. Remember, Jesus offers you and me the same quality and abundance of life that He possesses. We are witness that Jesus fulfilled His purpose here on earth. He destroyed the works of the devil, which include sin, sickness, demonic torment, poverty, destruction, deception, and fear. Jesus became the solution by providing salvation for sin, healing for sickness, freedom from the demonic, truth to set people free of lies, abundant life, and genuine love, which removes fear and judgment.

The problem comes when people decide what is good and evil independent of what God says in His Word and in relationship with Him. Doing so sets them on a course of destruction. In Joshua 24:15 (ESV), God admonished the people to *"choose this day whom you will serve."* The word "choose" in Hebrew is the image of plotting a ship's course. Moving into your purpose and destiny begins with your choice to "plot your course" toward God and to cooperate with His direction and development in your life. Jesus lived His purpose to provide freedom for us, but we must activate our faith and believe in Him to complete His perfect work within us.

Declaration

As Jesus fulfilled His purpose, I will fulfill mine. I will choose to serve the Lord this day and every day of my life.

Activation

In what ways have you allowed God to assist you in plotting your course? In what ways have you resisted His help?

Journal about the day you chose to connect with God and follow Him. Include the people who were influences in your life at the time. Write a letter thanking them for their contribution to your life.

_____

_____

_____

_____

_____

_____

_____

_____

_____

_____

_____

_____

_____

_____

Jesus Activated Grace for Empowerment and Timing

And taking the five loaves and the two fish, he looked up
to heaven and said a blessing and broke the loaves and
gave them to the disciples to set before the people. And he
divided the two fish among them all (Mark 6:41, ESV).

...He has sent me to proclaim liberty to the captives and recovering
of sight to the blind, to set at liberty those who are oppressed,
to proclaim the year of the Lord's favor (Luke 4:18-19, ESV).

Jesus faced challenges while living out His purpose and learned to choose God's view and opinion over His own. To do that, He exalted the eyes of His heart over His natural view. That strategy provided the capability to access unlimited resources to meet every need—and you have that same capability. In Mark 6:41 (above), the original language reads, *"He looked into heaven and recovered His sight."* That phrase, *"recovered sight,"* is the same as in Luke 4:18 (above): *"recovering of sight to the blind."* Jesus saw the need in the natural and understood His limitation, so He looked to the Father. He recovered His ability to see the unlimited resources of the Kingdom of Heaven then activated the miracle of multiplying food. Jesus teaches us to take the limits off our situation and see the opportunities and resources available to fulfill our purpose.

Jesus learned to activate grace for empowerment and timing in walking out His purpose. In John 7, when the Jews tried to kill Him, He said it was not yet His time. He knew it was His purpose to die for each of us, but He wanted God's perfect plan, which included the right time. God provides for every part of your purpose; you never need to spend time guessing what He means. He will tell you His plans when you ask.

Declaration

By following Jesus' example, I will consult the Lord before making decisions and taking actions. I will trust God to open my eyes to His unlimited resources.

Activation

Jesus modeled a lifestyle of stopping amid activity to hear from God before acting. Do you feel empowered to stop and ask for guidance before making decisions too? Why or why not?

Journal about a time you got the timing on a word exactly right. Are there also times you have gotten the timing wrong? Ask the Lord to show you the best method to better understand His perfect timing.

_____

_____

_____

_____

_____

_____

_____

_____

_____

_____

_____

_____

_____

Jesus' Example Is Encouragement in Your Purpose

But we see Jesus, who was made a little lower than the angels, for the suffering of death crowned with glory and honor, that He, by the grace of God, might taste death for everyone (Hebrews 2:9, NKJV).

Jesus was fully man and fully God, and without His Father's empowerment, the Cross would have been impossible to face. Jesus tasted death for every person by the grace of God. It was through communication with the Father that He received the grace to carry the Cross, become sin, and endure the devastating separation. In becoming sin, Jesus took on the curse of the law and allowed God's grace to work in you, making it possible to do what you can't do in your own strength or ability.

There are many more examples of Jesus living out His purpose that we can learn and grow from. Jesus came to reveal the Father and to show people what God was really like. He said that if people knew Him, they would have known the Father (John 8:19). After Jesus' resurrection, He commissioned His disciples with the same tasks the Father had given Him. In the same way the Father had sent Him, Jesus was sending them—and us.

You have the privilege and honor to reveal your heavenly Father to the world and be a problem solver who influences society. The way to do that is to live out your God-given purpose, trusting He has given you the gifts and the grace to fulfill it.

Declaration

I am immeasurably grateful for the price Jesus paid for me. I will live my life honoring the Father to the world.

Activation

How do you reveal God to the people around you? In what ways does your life speak of the glory of God even if you are not able to speak openly?

Journal your gratitude when you think about Jesus tasting death for you. Does Jesus being fully human change the image you hold in your mind of Him?

_____

_____

_____

_____

_____

_____

_____

_____

_____

_____

_____

_____

_____

_____

Fear Is a Tactic of the Enemy to Stop Purpose

There is no fear in love [dread does not exist]. But perfect (complete, full-grown) love drives out fear, because fear involves [the expectation of divine] punishment, so the one who is afraid [of God's judgment] is not perfected in love [has not grown into a sufficient understanding of God's love] (1 John 4:18, AMP).

Fear is a tactic of the enemy meant to stop us from fulfilling God's purpose in our lives. This verse in 1 John 4 is the first step and foundation for living a life free of fear. The bottom line is that you need to gain a strong understanding of God's love for you. Everything springs from there. Could this be the key to overcoming the fear of failure, fear of rejection, and more? The answer is a resounding, "Yes!" With an understanding of God's unconditional love, you will be able to exalt the Word of God over your thoughts, fears, imaginations, and eventually any unhealthy behaviors you have developed.

God is love; and as your loving Father, He will not break your heart or bring harm to you in any way. He will never give up on you, and He wants the best for you in every area of your life. God does not place demands on you. Rather,

He wants you to relate to Him out of love, not fear. His thoughts toward you are loving, positive, and kind—He will never abandon or let you down. In response, you make the choice to love Him and trust Him. Perfect love displaces fear. Fear simply cannot exist where there is love.

Declaration

Today I am determined to understand the unconditional love of God for me. I will not allow fear to crowd out the love of God in my mind and heart.

Activation

In what areas of your life are you experiencing fear that you have not been able to overcome? Take time to be still to hear the Lord speaking words of love to you today.

Do you know how much God loves you? Journal your thoughts about God's love—not His love in general, but specifically for you.

_____

_____

_____

_____

_____

_____

_____

_____

_____

_____

_____

_____

_____

_____

God Does Not Want You to Live with Fear

Blessed is the one who fears the Lord always, but whoever
hardens his heart will fall into calamity (Proverbs 28:14, ESV).

Fearing the Lord doesn't mean to be afraid of Him. Not at all. We have all grown up with our own concept of the fear of God; and if you are like me, it was not a positive one. I had the thought that God may become upset and "bonk" me over the head when I made a mistake or did something wrong. Studies show that a person's greatest fear is that of the unknown. It makes sense that if you're not quite sure of God's character or His love for you, it would open the door for fear to have a place in your life.

The word "fear" in the Old Testament carries the idea of awe, respect, and love that results in worship. God wants you to have an awe of Him that results in worship, not fear. The fear of the Lord is not a negative concept or reason for concern; it is just misunderstood. It is not a contradiction in the Word when you see commands to *"fear not,"* and commands to *"fear God."* The Old Testament describes the covenant nature of God, where He tells people not to fear.

Jesus appeared to His disciples after His resurrection and told them not to fear. God does not want you to experience fear in your heart. He does want you to have a personal relationship with Him and trust His Word, knowing you are loved and accepted.

Declaration

I am blessed because I respect and love the Lord God. I will not harden my heart—I will trust God's Word.

Activation

In your own words, describe the difference between the fear, awe, respect, and reverence for God versus His command to not fear.

Journal about your concept of the fear of God. Have you been afraid of God rather than in awe of Him? Ask Him to show you the difference.

_____

_____

_____

_____

_____

_____

_____

_____

_____

_____

_____

_____

_____

_____

Take Every Thought Captive

For the weapons of our warfare are not of the flesh but have divine
power to destroy strongholds. We destroy arguments and every
lofty opinion raised against the knowledge of God, and take every
thought captive to obey Christ (2 Corinthians 10:4-5, ESV).

Fear brings worry and anxiety, and keeps you up at
night, imagining things that haven't yet happened—
and may never happen—in your life. This Scripture
passage in 2 Corinthians 10 is one that has helped me in
this area. I used to think I needed to grab myself by the
collar and bring my thoughts into the obedience of Christ,
feeling as though I was in trouble with the principal. But
God gave me a revelation one day as I was reading His
Word. I realized that He isn't scolding me, He's loving me
and telling me to cast down that fearful thought because
it's crowding out the knowledge of God in my mind and
heart.

Take, for example, being afraid while raising your
children. God is saying that every time you have a fearful thought about your child, reject it. Next, bring every
thought into captivity to the obedience of Christ. I thought
I needed to carry condemnation for my thoughts and do a
"penance" to be free. But now I know that when I bring

my fearful thoughts into the obedience of Christ and exalt what He says in His Word about my child as truth—my child is blessed, full of peace, and obedient to the Lord—over the fearful thoughts, He brings peace to my situation.

Declaration

Today, I will take every thought captive to the obedience of Christ. I will believe the Word of God over any thought that frightens me.

Activation

How do you practice taking thoughts captive to the obedience of Christ? In what ways do you allow fearful thoughts to crowd out the knowledge of the love of God?

List every time you are fearful (even in small ways) during the day. At the end of the day, ask the Lord how you could have taken those thoughts captive in the moment. He will answer you.

_____

_____

_____

_____

_____

_____

_____

_____

_____

_____

_____

_____

_____

_____

Fear Not People's Reproach

Listen to Me, you who know righteousness, you people in
whose heart is My law: Do not fear the reproach of men,
nor be afraid of their insults (Isaiah 51:7, NKJV).

O ne of the most common hindrances to fulfilling
your destiny is the fear of people. It causes you to
identify more with others' opinions than God's
opinions and to irrationally worry about how you're per-
ceived by other people. Fear of people can cause you to step
outside of your purpose and destiny in God just to please
others. This is an indication that you're not trusting Him
to bring promotion or right connections. Instead, you're
putting your trust in people to do what only God can do.

In this verse in Isaiah 51, God is reminding us of who we
are and telling us to *"not fear the reproach of men"* because
He knew we would deal with others' opinions. One thing
you can be sure of as you travel through life is that not
everyone will like you. As you courageously step into your
purpose and destiny, there will be resistance. But the Bible
says you have favor and good understanding in the sight of
"both God and people" (Proverbs 3:4, NLT). You can stand
on that promise.

Of course, you care about and love people, don't want to be rude toward anyone, and always show the love of God. But be aware, if God has a call on your life and He has given you an assignment to complete, you will be criticized. Thankfully, God says we don't need to fear the opinion of others, and that is good news.

Declaration

Because God's words are in my heart, I do not need to fear the insults around me. There is a call on my life, and I will approach and live it boldly.

Activation

You know that the enemy is the accuser of believers. How can you separate the accuser (a person) from the accusation (a tool of the enemy)?

Journal about a few interactions where you felt accused or misunderstood. Include both your reactions and an ideal response. Ask the Lord to help with your next interaction.

_____

_____

_____

_____

_____

_____

_____

_____

_____

_____

_____

_____

_____

DAY 20

Fear Is Defeated in the Mind

You are of your father the devil, and the desires of your father
you want to do. He was a murderer from the beginning, and
does not stand in the truth, because there is no truth in him.
When he speaks a lie, he speaks from his own resources,
for he is a liar and the father of it (John 8:44, NKJV).

Fear is defeated in the mind. Fear is thinking about something that could happen but isn't actually happening and may never happen. If you logically examine what is causing you fear, worry, and anxiety, it's almost a 100 percent guarantee that it is based in your mind. This means that between your ears, you have created a world based in non-reality, like playing a movie in your mind. It's a ploy of the enemy to get you to believe a lie and stop you from fulfilling your purpose. This is not something to be condemned about but to learn from, so you can take the Word of God as truth and trust Him completely.

Developing a process to filter your thoughts begins with identifying a lie and understanding the source of fear and lies. John 10:10 (AMP) tells us, *"The thief comes only in order to steal and kill and destroy. I [Jesus] came that they may have and enjoy life, and have it in abundance [to the full, till it overflows]."*

In which camp are your thoughts? There is one camp that will eventually steal, kill, or destroy you, which is the enemy's camp. The enemy's language is accusatory, destructive, and negative. The enemy has no truth in him, so thoughts from him can only be lies.

Then there is the camp of "life more abundant," which is Jesus' camp. Jesus' language blesses, and is merciful and life giving. Jesus is the Prince of Peace, so thoughts from Him can only bring peace.

Declaration

My life is solidly based in the camp of the Prince of Peace. This day I will walk in peace, putting aside all thoughts from the enemy.

Activation

In what camp are your thoughts? In what ways do you allow fear to create movies in your mind?

Take time to list some thoughts or consistent thought patterns you had today. Determine if those thoughts were generally in the enemy's camp or Jesus' camp.

_____

_____

_____

_____

_____

_____

_____

_____

_____

_____

_____

_____

_____

_____

_____

_____

God Puts Fear under Our Feet

Therefore, I remind you to stir up the gift of God which is in you through the laying on of my hands. For God has not given us a spirit of fear, but of power and of love and of a sound mind (2 Timothy 1:6-7, NKJV).

If you feel anxious, worried, and stressed, you're entertaining thoughts from the enemy, and all he can do is lie. I have learned to connect fear-filled thoughts to a lie from the enemy. Once you make that connection, you can reject the lie and speak the truth of God's Word regarding the situation. Once the thought is identified as a lie, you can apply 2 Corinthians 10:5, take that thought captive, and then replace it with truth. This is literally how I learned to process thoughts because I am so logical. I need to see it in the Word, then know how to apply it. Simply put:

- Fear is from the enemy.
- There is no truth in the enemy.
- Therefore, there is no truth in fear.
- Does this thought bring fear?
- If so, it is not from the Lord.
- Exchange that thought for a promise in God's Word.

- Agree with the Word and turn away from fear.
- What you agree with is what has power in your life.

In our world today, there's a vast amount of conflicting information, causing thoughts of fear, worry, uncertainty, and anxiety. God knew we would struggle with fear, so He gave us a way out. He addresses fear and puts it under our feet. over and over throughout His Word. He did that for us. Fear is not only able to be defeated, it is *already* defeated.

Declaration

Knowing fear-filled thoughts come from the enemy, I will not entertain them. I will agree with God's Word and turn away from fear.

Activation

How good are you at identifying a lie when you hear it?
Describe your success at utilizing the tools God gave you to
combat fear; namely, power, love, and a sound mind.

Spend a week using this system to process your thoughts.
Journal the results. Watch what the Lord will do.

_____

_____

_____

_____

_____

_____

_____

_____

_____

_____

_____

_____

_____

_____

_____

Shattering Glass Ceilings

Out of my deep anguish and pain I prayed, and God, you helped
me as a father. You came to my rescue and broke open the way
into a beautiful and broad place. Now I know, Lord, that you
are for me, and I will never fear what man can do to me. For you
stand beside me as my hero who rescues me. I've seen with my
own eyes the defeat of my enemies. I've triumphed over them
all! Lord, it is so much better to trust in you to save me than to
put my confidence in someone else (Psalm 118:5-8, TPT).

A "glass ceiling" is an invisible hindrance that you
may not be fully aware of, intended to limit your
success. It is another tool the enemy uses to distract or derail you from fulfilling your purpose. Limitations
can be placed on you from the outside, but more often
they come from the inside. Much of what affects your life
begins in your mind, like fear. Daily learning to see yourself
as God sees you and remembering what value He places
on you will give you the courage to push through any glass
ceiling you face. Your loving heavenly Father sent Jesus to
pay your ransom, wash you clean as new-fallen snow, and
open endless opportunities to you.

Life is full of experiences—some good and some bad—
that mold your future. There are times when you may carry

those past experiences into new parts of your life. Good experiences can bring joy, hope, and life, but bad experiences bring fear, pain, and lies. The latter can impose limits that you unconsciously submit to. No matter where limitations come from, God is the One who removes them. He rescues you and fights for you as a father and a hero. He is on your side and wants the best for you.

Declaration

God is my Hero, and He will defeat my enemies. Limitations will no longer keep me from breaking through to a beautiful and broad place.

Activation

What glass ceilings have you been aware of in your life? Have you been fighting and railing against them, or have you decided life is just that way? Why?

As the Lord reveals limitations to you, make a list of them, and watch Him rescue you each time.

_____

_____

_____

_____

_____

_____

_____

_____

_____

_____

_____

_____

_____

_____

_____

DAY 23

Past Experiences Can Affect Your Future

Thus says the Lord, who makes a way in the sea, a path in the mighty waters, who brings forth chariot and horse, army and warrior; they lie down, they cannot rise, they are extinguished, quenched like a wick: "Remember not the former things, nor consider the things of old. Behold, I am doing a new thing; now it springs forth, do you not perceive it? I will make a way in the wilderness and rivers in the desert" (Isaiah 43:16-19, ESV).

Past experiences are another form of limitation that can distract or derail you from your purpose. If you've had a bad experience in a relationship, such as a marriage ending, a business failing, or a child rebelling, you may be tempted to apply your past experience of failure to your current situation and approach a new relationship with a bias God doesn't want you to have. It is not the event that does the damage, it is the significance you attach to the event and what you believe. If you have not dealt with the past and renewed your mind to the Word of God, you can take the expectation of failure into your new circumstances.

In this passage in Isaiah 43, the Lord was encouraging Israel that He won't hold their past against them. Israel had a past full of mistakes, failures, and bad decisions, but God was not looking backward, only forward. Think about the difficult past experiences of your life. The Lord is telling you, "I am God, and I have created everything." Then He says to forget the past, and He encourages you that these things will not rise again. He's doing a brand-new thing, not the old thing again. Be encouraged. You're not destined to repeat the same mistakes or failures over and over in your life. God has a plan to bring good even from your mistakes.

Declaration

I break any old thought patterns and negative inner vows I have spoken and believe God is going to do a new thing in my life in the name of Jesus. Thank You, God, for rivers in the desert.

Activation

What in your past has possibly created a mindset, a stronghold, or an expectation of falling short of God's best for you? Have you made any negative vows because of a past event, such as not trusting people after you were hurt?

Journal through some past experiences that still affect how you think. Ask the Lord to help you forget them and do a new thing.

_____

_____

_____

_____

_____

_____

_____

_____

_____

_____

_____

_____

_____

Forget the Past Because God Already Has

Now listen, daughter, pay attention, and forget about your past. Put behind you every attachment to the familiar, even those who once were close to you! (Psalm 45:10, TPT)

God's commandments are not negative do's and don'ts; in Hebrew, this conveys the idea of pre-scriptions for health. His commandment to forget the past is for your own personal health because He knows negative viewpoints are destructive. God is telling you not to get comfortable looking backward; rather, turn your face toward the future He has set before you. The enemy loves to bring up your past, and he'll do it at times when you are tired, down on yourself, or confused. But God says to forget the past—He has forgotten it—and look to the future purpose He has designed for you.

I lost my first husband without any warning, and it was traumatic. But if I had continued to relive that trauma in my mind, I would not have been able to move forward with joy. God will transform those things that happened that were meant to cause harm (Romans 8:28). As you cooperate with Him, exalt Him, and love Him, you'll start to see the life He has for you in His Word. You don't need to relive past trauma. You can look at things the way God sees them, and the past becomes a distant memory used for your good. Today, I can look back on what happened and see how God has taken what the enemy meant for my harm and turned it for good in my life. If I can do this, so can you.

Declaration

God has put my past away and forgotten it; I will do the same. I will look to the future He has prepared for me.

Activation

If you have a trauma you can't seem to get past, have you allowed fear to attach to that trauma? If so, do an exchange with Jesus. Give Him your fear(s) and receive from Him what you need. For example, tell Jesus you're giving Him your fear of rejection, then receive love, acceptance, and value from Him.

How do you feel about the transformation God does from something meant for harm to something good? Journal your thoughts and your thanksgiving.

_____

_____

_____

_____

_____

_____

_____

_____

_____

_____

_____

_____

Everything about You Is Made New

Therefore, if anyone is in Christ, he is a new creation. The old has passed away; behold, the new has come. ...in Christ God was reconciling the world to himself, not counting their trespasses against them, and entrusting to us the message of reconciliation. ...For our sake he made him to be sin who knew no sin, so that in him we might become the righteousness of God (2 Corinthians 5:17,19,21, ESV).

Many times, your past sins can distract or deter you from fulfilling your purpose. Look at your past—no matter the situation—and determine whether you have dealt with it through the blood of Jesus. Maybe you never had a true revelation of what God has done in your life. Do you hold on to past sin and allow it to limit you because you feel you're not worthy? This area sneaks up on people who don't realize they are still holding themselves to past sin. When you're able to release this, you'll have so much life open up to you.

This passage in 2 Corinthians 5 says you have become an entirely new creation. All that is related to the old order has vanished, and all things are made new. That truth is so powerful. Does it mean only some things are new? No, that's not what God said. He said everything is fresh and new, and you are enfolded in Christ. You are a new creature. Praise God, His cleansing is continual.

When you are born again, you receive everything in the spirit. Legally, everything is paid for—but you and I must respond and receive it, which is a very active thing. It requires humility to exalt what God says is true over how we feel or what our circumstances indicate. Jesus has made your sins as white as snow, and nothing can take that from you. You need only to trust and believe Him.

Declaration

Through Christ, I am a new creation. All my old sins and mistakes have passed away, and I am free.

Activation

How have past sins affected your ability to walk in happiness or success? What limitations have you experienced?

List on paper the sins from your past that make you feel unworthy. Thank the Lord as you acknowledge His work that cleansed you once and for all. Then, light the list on fire; as you watch it burn, remember that He has removed them permanently for your sake.

_____

_____

_____

_____

_____

_____

_____

_____

_____

_____

_____

_____

_____

_____

_____

DAY 26

The Holy Spirit Will Lead You into All Truth

And I will ask the Father, and He will give you another Helper (Comforter, Advocate, Intercessor—Counselor, Strengthener, Standby), to be with you forever—the Spirit of Truth, whom the world cannot receive [and take to its heart] because it does not see Him or know Him, but you know Him because He (the Holy Spirit) remains with you continually and will be in you (John 14:16-17, AMP).

Let me ask you this: What lies are you believing today? What have you allowed to take root in your mind that causes you to agree with the enemy instead of the truth of the Word? Do you understand that what Jesus did was enough? If you agree with something negative in your life instead of the truth, you are the deciding factor. Your life will go in the direction of the lie you believe. You need to recognize that those things outside of God's will are lies, and then find the truth of what God says about those things instead. You can choose to take your mind, will, and emotions and line them up with the truth. This is a key to walking in God's purpose for your life and removing that glass ceiling. And we have the best help available to us through the Holy Spirit.

When you recognize lies and limitations and where they come from, you can begin breaking through your glass ceiling. If a limitation is holding you back, exalt the Word of God and what He says about you. Take the process outlined for fear and apply it to each of the areas of limitation you identify in your life. I want you to know that the Father sees you as an absolutely amazing person with outstanding potential—because He sees you and me through the blood of Jesus.

Declaration

What Jesus did on the Cross was enough. God sees me through the blood of Jesus, and I will cast down any thought that says otherwise.

Activation

Ask the Lord to show you where you may be believing a lie in a specific area of your life.

Dig into the Word to see what God says about you. Then list anything that speaks against the way God sees you and start to dispel those lies.

_____

_____

_____

_____

_____

_____

_____

_____

_____

_____

_____

_____

_____

_____

_____

_____

Believe What God Says about Every Situation

When pride comes [boiling up with an arrogant attitude of self-importance], then come dishonor and shame, but with the humble [the teachable who have been chiseled by trial and who have learned to walk humbly with God] there is wisdom and soundness of mind (Proverbs 11:2, AMP).

Typically, we think of pride as magnifying ourselves and boasting of our strengths, which can be an issue. But what's more of a problem and causes more of a glass ceiling is exalting our abilities, *or lack of them*, over what Jesus did. If I took a test but didn't do very well, I might decide not to take that test again. My emotions say, *I can't do it because I didn't pass it last time. I'm just not that smart.* But the Word of God says I have the mind of Christ. Which is true? Without pride, I can set aside my shortcomings, my past experiences, and my natural limitations, and believe what God says. Pride can mean believing your own limitations or what's only possible in the natural instead of believing what God says about the circumstance.

No matter your situation, you need to know that you can't overcome it without the Lord. Give it the best you have, but rely on the Lord to complete it and bring success. Stop looking at your own ability. People who depend on themselves come quickly to the end of themselves. I don't want to have a glass ceiling that stops at my own natural talents and abilities. I want to honor God by receiving all He has for my life. A big part of that is seeing myself the way He sees me—knowing there are no limits on my life because He is near. When I don't depend on myself for results, there is peace and courage.

Declaration

I will no longer submit to pride and allow my limitations to win the day. I will do my very best and rely on God to bring the results.

Activation

In what way does your self-talk promote negative, discouraging thoughts? Positive, encouraging thoughts? Do you give up on things because of how you feel?

Journal about a time when you were tempted to give up. Whether you did or not, ask the Lord to speak to you about that situation.

_____

_____

_____

_____

_____

_____

_____

_____

_____

_____

_____

_____

_____

_____

_____

_____

Discover Your Purpose

And we know [with great confidence] that God [who is deeply concerned about us] causes all things to work together [as a plan] for good for those who love God, to those who are called according to His plan and purpose (Romans 8:28, AMP).

It is God's privilege to conceal things and the king's privilege to discover them (Proverbs 25:2, NLT).

It's encouraging to learn that God has designed you with a unique purpose and destiny, but just knowing it's "out there" isn't enough. It's your privilege to get with God to discover your purpose. He designed your purpose specifically for you, and He already knows what it is. He is deeply concerned about you, and He wants you to know the purpose for your life as much as you want to discover His plan. Get Him involved, and together you can uncover and discover your purpose.

When the temptation comes to feel that you have wasted years and too many careers without knowing your purpose, remember Romans 8:28. What a comfort it is to have the confidence that God will make all things work together for good. Be encouraged! You can look back on your life, remove the things you know weren't from God, and see how He cared for you and led you through the years when you didn't realize it.

It's a beautiful thread that God has sewn through your life to get you where you are today, ready to step into your destiny. Take a quick look back to see how God was leading you, and pay attention to the things you learned. They are going to be valuable in discovering your purpose.

Declaration

I am called according to His purpose. God is causing all things to work together for my good.

Activation

When looking at your life, what activities or jobs made you feel the most "alive" and successful?

Take time to write out your dreams and your hopes. Pray over them and discuss them with someone who believes in you.

_____

_____

_____

_____

_____

_____

_____

_____

_____

_____

_____

_____

_____

_____

_____

_____

_____

You Have Been Given Gifts for Your Unique Purpose

A man's gift [given in love or courtesy] makes room for him
and brings him before great men (Proverbs 18:16, AMP).

Every good thing given and every perfect gift is from above;
it comes down from the Father of lights [the Creator and
Sustainer of the heavens], in whom there is no variation
[no rising or setting] or shadow cast by His turning [for
He is perfect and never changes] (James 1:17, AMP).

Your gift is the special endowment and grace that
God has given you. For instance, it may be easy
for you to look at a complex problem and immediately see how to solve it. You may have a beautiful voice,
while there are others of us who can't carry a tune. Learn to
recognize the gifts and talents God has given you, and be
aware that your purpose is probably tied to those gifts. It's
part of the uniqueness that is *the you* created by God. You
will likely have many gifts on your list, and He promises to
give you even more. However, only a few will stand out as
the core reason you do the things you do.

God thinks bigger than you do. He says His ways are
not your ways, but you can renew your mind to see what

He sees. Thankfully, our steps are ordered by the Lord (Psalm 37:23), which gives us confidence.

Sometimes things in life don't make sense. You need confidence that He has it all under control. God knows what is ahead of you, and He's already there, ordering your steps. As a child of God, you can seek Him and follow His voice and know that He has your whole path laid out. Isn't this good?

Declaration

My gifts will make room for me and bring me before important people. My steps are ordered by God.

Activation

What can you accomplish easily, but is often difficult for others? Under what circumstances do you quickly see solutions and feel compelled to take action?

List in your notes what you think are your core gifts and begin asking the Lord how He can use them in your life.

_____

_____

_____

_____

_____

_____

_____

_____

_____

_____

_____

_____

_____

_____

_____

_____

DAY 30

Your Purpose Will Energize You

Whatever you do, work heartily, as for the Lord and not for men, knowing that from the Lord you will receive the inheritance as your reward. You are serving the Lord Christ (Colossians 3:23-24, ESV).

What do you love to do? What can you work on for hours and end up more energized than tired? This is another clue to your purpose. God says He gives us the desires of our heart when we seek Him. He's not going to call you to spend your life doing something you hate. You can trust that those things you enjoy doing, which also line up with the Word, are from God. For me, I can work for hours staging a home. I worked on a home one day for fourteen hours! By the end of the day, I was physically tired, but I was not exhausted or drained. That was possible because I was working out of my purpose. I loved every minute of fulfilling a purpose deeper than an individual job or assignment.

There's a supernatural energy that comes to us from the Spirit of God when we live out His purpose. That energy is available to you. Think about what energizes you. It might not be related to anything you're involved with currently. Many times, jobs or careers are chosen based on how successful or profitable they appear to be. Rarely are passions or contentment considered in choosing the direction for a career path. Even if you don't know your purpose yet, the Lord is working on your behalf, preparing you for the future.

Declaration

I commit to do everything for the Lord. I have an inheritance and reward reserved for me.

Activation

What energizes you? What routine tasks bring you joy?

Put these in BIG letters in your notes. You are getting closer to discovering your purpose.

_____

_____

_____

_____

_____

_____

_____

_____

_____

_____

_____

_____

_____

_____

_____

_____

DAY 31

God Assures Your Gifts Will Be Appreciated

This is what the Lord, your Redeemer, the Holy One of Israel says, "I am the Lord your God, who teaches you to profit (benefit), who leads you in the way that you should go. Oh, that you had paid attention to My commandments! Then your peace and prosperity would have been like a [flowing] river, and your righteousness [the holiness and purity of the nation] like the [abundant] waves of the sea" (Isaiah 48:17-18, AMP).

I t's amazing how you can wake up one day and decide you're not being paid enough, and you're underappreciated or undervalued. I have lived this myself, and I realize now it's a warning sign. When I hear people say they're not paid enough for what they're expected to do, it is a signal for me to ask, "Why are you feeling this way?" Usually that feeling is masking a different problem. It's quite possible that they are no longer working from a healthy place in their purpose. It could mean they have mastered their current task, which initially matched up to their purpose. Or they may just need another challenge to continue to be fulfilled.

If you're starting to feel underappreciated, ask this question: "Am I working to please people or to please the

Lord?" It's a good way to check whether you have gotten off-track and have started pursuing recognition or money, which can creep up very subtly. Discontentment can also be an indication that there's a season of change or a transition coming your way. It might be challenging, and you may feel fearful about the next season, but you can know that your heavenly Father will lead you into something greater. The Lord is always about growth, multiplication, fruitfulness, and profit. He'll direct your life to the next level of grace, the next level of peace, and the next level of success.

Declaration

The God of the universe teaches me and leads me in the way I should go. I will not be afraid for the future; I will walk in peace.

Activation

Think about a job you held where you were initially content, but then later became discontent. What was the last project or assignment you mastered before becoming discontent?

Journal about a time you felt underappreciated or underpaid. Walk through the situation with the Lord and let Him speak to you.

_____

_____

_____

_____

_____

_____

_____

_____

_____

_____

_____

_____

_____

DAY 32

God's Purpose Will Succeed

The blessing of the Lord–it makes [truly] rich, and
He adds no sorrow with it [neither does toiling
increase it] (Proverbs 10:22, AMP Classic).

For after all these things the Gentiles seek. For your heavenly
Father knows that you need all these things. But seek first
the kingdom of God and His righteousness, and all these
things shall be added to you (Matthew 6:32-33, NKJV).

When you focus on God's purpose for your life, you can expect the blessing of the Lord with no sorrow. There are movie stars, music stars, executives, politicians, and even pastors who hold on to their talent as their own. They seem to have achieved what everyone strives after. But seeking people's approval and positions without God's purpose leads to an empty and disappointing life. Strive after His purpose, and all the things the world pursues will be given to you, including peace. Evaluate your job, career, and activity choices through the filter of the Word of God and the direction of the purpose He has placed on your life. He will gladly guide you to the best place for you.

God says in Matthew 25:29 that as you value His gifts and apply them wisely, He will add more gifts to you. If you don't apply His gifts wisely, He says that even what you have will be taken away. I don't want to be in that situation; I want to be found faithful. Proverbs 19:21 (NLT) assures us that *"You can make many plans, but the Lord's purpose will prevail."* Not "maybe," not "might," but His purpose *will* prevail, or succeed. When you line yourself up with God's purpose, success is imminent.

Declaration

I will seek the Kingdom of God and His righteousness in all my endeavors. I will trust that the Lord's purpose for my life will succeed.

Activation

What current jobs, businesses, or activities do you feel are in line with God's purpose for your life? Are there any you feel are not in line with your purpose?

List all the volunteer, pro bono, and community activities, as well as your job. Ask the Lord if there are things you should discontinue or things you should add.

_____

_____

_____

_____

_____

_____

_____

_____

_____

_____

_____

_____

_____

_____

_____

_____

The Bible Is Full of Promises to Help Fulfill Your Purpose

Christ redeemed us from the curse of the law by becoming a curse for us—for it is written, "Cursed is everyone who is hanged on a tree"—so that in Christ Jesus the blessing of Abraham might come to the Gentiles, so that we might receive the promised Spirit through faith (Galatians 3:13-14, ESV).

The blessings of Abraham are vast and far-reaching. God already has blessed your family, your name, your spiritual life, your home, and your children. He promises protection, provision, authority, blessing, and peace. You can be fruitful, righteous, and a blessing to the nations. You qualify for all the blessings of Abraham through the blood of Jesus. All this and more is available for you because Jesus has already made provision. All you need to do to receive is believe.

Galatians explains that God freed us from the curse and positioned us to receive all the promises and blessings He made in times past. The covenant was with Jesus and the promises made to Him. Because we are in Him, we qualify to participate in the covenant. We have a covenant of peace, sealed by the blood of Jesus—and our actions will not change the covenant. We have the Word of God; it is not a list of rules, but a manual for living an abundant life. It's a treasure chest of gifts and promises to help fulfill your purpose. In the Bible you'll find answers to every question and tools for every situation. There's power to overcome right at your fingertips.

Declaration

Through Jesus Christ, I no longer live under a curse—I live under the promises of faith.

Activation

What do you know about the blessings of Abraham? How does realizing that they are available to you affect your daily life?

List the promises you hold on to daily. Take time to find promises you haven't been aware of and add them to your list.

_____

_____

_____

_____

_____

_____

_____

_____

_____

_____

_____

_____

_____

You Are Not a Bother—You Are a Blessing

And I will make of you a great nation, and I will bless you and make
your name great, so that you will be a blessing (Genesis 12:2, ESV).

God has already provided the tools we need to fulfill our purpose, which are available if we know about them. I love this promise because God says He has made me to be a blessing. His Word combats one of the things I hear frequently from women—whether single, divorced, or widowed—which is that they don't want to be a bother to anyone. I can't tell you how many conversations I have been in like the one I had with a friend the other day. She was helping with my hair and makeup and said, "Karen, anytime you need help, please let me know." I heard myself say, "I just don't want to be a bother." But I need to stop thinking that way and understand that I'm not a bother; I'm a blessing.

When you feel like a bother, you walk timidly into a room, you don't call people for help, and you don't want to disturb anyone. God doesn't want that for you. He wants you to understand that even in a crowd, He's already declared you to be a blessing.

Try walking into your next situation with this understanding. I know when I start to work or interact with people—feeling that I'm a bother and not a blessing—my actions unconsciously follow my feelings. Always remember, you are a blessing because He made you to be a blessing.

Declaration

I am a blessing. I was made to be a blessing to those around me through the promises of God. I will walk into every situation, knowing that I bring blessing with me.

Activation

Do you know that you are a blessing, or do you feel like a bother to those around you?

Journal about the interactions of one day. Determine if you felt like a blessing in each interaction and why.

_____

_____

_____

_____

_____

_____

_____

_____

_____

_____

_____

_____

_____

_____

_____

Sharing in the Giving Heart of God

I will bless those who bless you, and him who dishonors
you I will curse, and in you all the families of the
earth shall be blessed (Genesis 12:3, ESV).

When people help me, bless me, speak good things over me, give me gifts, or spend time with me, God says He will bless them in return. Even if I don't have the opportunity to thank them, I am grateful to God that because they chose to bless me, He is going to bless them. I love this because it allows me to share in the heart of God as I fulfill my purpose. He rewards people who bless His children. God is looking to bless all those around us.

You are not under the curse, and God is not in the cursing business, and there's something in this verse in Genesis 12 that shows how well God is looking out for you. If someone says or does something unkind, you can know that He cares about it, and He takes it personally. He is just, so you can go to Him and trust He will get you through difficult times.

All the families of the earth are going to be blessed through those who belong to Jesus Christ. God has a plan to expand His Kingdom on earth through your family; and as you walk in your purpose, you get to partner with Him in spreading His Kingdom. His influence will reach the ends of the earth through your family.

Declaration

All the families of the earth will be blessed through my family. I trust God to walk me through difficult times with blessing.

Activation

God is always looking for a way to bless. What are some ways you can bless others as you go through your day—even in casual interactions? It may be a smile, kind words, listening, showing patience, and more.

Set one day aside to bless as many people as you interact with. Journal your feelings, reactions, and results.

_____

_____

_____

_____

_____

_____

_____

_____

_____

_____

_____

_____

_____

_____

DAY 36

God Is a Shield of Protection

For you bless the righteous, O Lord; you cover him
with favor as with a shield (Psalm 5:12 ESV).

As you go through life, there can be some dangerous occasions. Many times your life of purpose
will include risks that can be physical, emotional,
financial, and spiritual. I had a situation where I was driving
just outside my workplace, and I felt a bump with my car. I
looked up, and it was a big buck. I just caught a glimpse of
it. Hitting a deer can be dangerous, but God protected me,
and the buck kept running. When I looked at the front of
my car, I saw that my headlights were completely pushed in.
People stopped me in the driveway of the building where
I work, concerned about what had happened. I said that I
hit a deer, but it was just a little bump. They were stunned
because it looked so serious, and I could have been injured.

When I called the insurance company and told them
what happened, I explained the damage, and they were
concerned I had whiplash or back issues. I told them I
was fine. God was my Shield. He's my Shield in the natural—and He's a Shield in the spiritual realm. When there
are times I am not sure if I am brave enough to step out
into something or I have a challenge I can't quite figure

out, God is my Shield. I know that I have His protection because of His promise.

Declaration

God is my Shield and Protector. I can be brave enough to face any challenge with the Lord by my side.

Activation

Think about some situations where you could have been injured in an accident but weren't or maybe avoided an accident altogether. Take a moment and praise God for His blessing and protection over your life.

Journal about a time when you saw the protection of the Lord in a powerful way. Ask the Lord to show you a time when you were not aware of His protection.

_____

_____

_____

_____

_____

_____

_____

_____

_____

_____

_____

_____

DAY 37

God Will Never Break His Covenant with You

And he believed the Lord, and he counted it to
him as righteousness (Genesis 15:6, ESV).

Come now, let us make a covenant, you and I. And let it be
a witness between you and me (Genesis 31:44, ESV).

Y ou are partnering with God in this life of purpose;
His presence will be an encouragement and comfort no matter what comes your way. He has made
you in right standing, which isn't based on your behavior
or because you're so smart. You are the righteousness of
God because you have received Jesus Christ. You can hold
your head high and come boldly to the throne of grace to
receive mercy and find grace to help in your time of need
(Hebrews 4:16). You can go to your Father, who is God
and has created the universe. He knows you; and when
He looks at you, He sees you as righteous as Jesus. That is
amazing! You can take His robe of righteousness and walk
on this earth as if you are sinless.

When God established a covenant with you through
Jesus Christ, it wasn't just for this moment. You can stand
on the Word and know that all the generations behind

you are going to be in covenant with God. I can have my grandchildren sit on my lap and tell them they are in covenant with a good Father. The Conrad lineage is changed forever because of the decision we made to follow Jesus. A covenant relationship is very serious to God. He will never break a covenant.

Declaration

I am righteous through Christ. I am in covenant with the One True God. I will walk through today knowing to whom I belong.

Activation

How confident are you in your relationship with the Lord? How confident are you that you are the righteousness of God?

List your children and grandchildren. Write the date when each one became a believer. If some haven't yet, stand on God's promise regarding your covenant family.

_____

_____

_____

_____

_____

_____

_____

_____

_____

_____

_____

_____

_____

_____

Trust Jesus to Bring Your Faith to Conclusion

Therefore, we also, since we are surrounded by so great a cloud
of witnesses, let us lay aside every weight, and the sin which so
easily ensnares us, and let us run with endurance the race that
is set before us, looking unto Jesus, the author and finisher of
our faith, who for the joy that was set before Him endured
the cross, despising the shame, and has sat down at the right
hand of the throne of God (Hebrews 12:1-2, NKJV).

You don't have to strive for enough faith to walk
in the purpose you have been given; God made
provision for you. These verses in Hebrews 12
explain that Jesus is actively involved in our faith from the
beginning to the end. Jesus is the *"author and finisher"* of
our faith. The definition of "author" in Greek is "captain."
That helps us understand that Jesus was the Originator of
our faith because He begins it, and then leads it as a captain leads a ship and its crew and cares for it and them. We
can trust Jesus to bring our faith to conclusion. This is so
wonderful!

When I feel that my faith is not as strong as it should
be, I lean into this Scripture and ask Jesus to make up any

lack in my faith and bring it to completion for me. Jesus, the Captain of our faith, watches over us, cares for us, and sustains us. God has so much reserved for you, and He is near to help you navigate your journey with purpose. He has made provision for you in every area of your life, and His Word is the manual for success. He has promises and blessings stored up for you that are astounding.

Declaration

Jesus is the Captain of my faith. I will ask Him to fill in the gaps where my faith is weak and supply me with courage to fulfill my purpose.

Activation

Describe a time when you found yourself trying to muster up enough faith to make it through a situation.

Journal about a day full of faith and courage. What happens when you have days that are not full of faith and courage? Ask the Lord for a daily dose of it.

_____

_____

_____

_____

_____

_____

_____

_____

_____

_____

_____

_____

_____

_____

God Is Invested in Your Success

And let us not grow weary of doing good, for in due season we
will reap, if we do not give up. So then, as we have opportunity,
let us do good to everyone, and especially to those who
are of the household of faith (Galatians 6:9-10, ESV).

Principles for success, whether personal or business
related, can ultimately be traced back to the Bible.
You will find that God is invested in your success,
and He provides you with all the tools, talents, and grace
you need to fulfill your purpose. Some of those tools are
good habits you can develop to strengthen your character,
and some are supernatural gifts you already possess but
didn't know you had.

For instance, have you ever had enthusiastic teachers
or colleagues change the atmosphere in the room because
their passion for the subject or confidence in the team
became contagious? Scripture indicates that enthusiasm
starts with delighting in the Lord and His Word (Psalm
112; read the whole chapter). As a leader of an organiza-
tion, team, or family, if you approach the office, a Zoom
call, or a family pow-wow with a lack of enthusiasm, how
can you expect the people around you to be encouraged
or upbeat?

With enthusiasm, you can overcome obstacles that would otherwise feel impossible. I want to encourage you to come with enthusiasm to your leadership role, whether in your family or with your colleagues. When you do, you will find that other people enjoy being around you, and they want to participate with you in bringing about a successful outcome. An enthusiastic attitude is contagious!

Declaration

I will not grow weary as I work to fulfill my purpose. I will influence and attract others with enthusiasm. I will be a change maker in my sphere of influence.

Activation

Think of a time when you knew the atmosphere needed to change in your office or home. Were you able to help with that change? If so, how?

Journal about a day with lots of interactions, whether in person or online. Include your thoughts on how each one could have gone differently with more enthusiasm.

_____

_____

_____

_____

_____

_____

_____

_____

_____

_____

_____

_____

_____

_____

_____

Walking Out Your Purpose Begins One Day at a Time

Do not be deceived: God is not mocked, for whatever
one sows, that will he also reap (Galatians 6:7, ESV).

Your life and success in your purpose is a result of what you do daily and begins one day at a time. Sometimes you don't want to hear that because, frankly, there are days you would really like to sit around and not accomplish much of anything. And occasionally is not a problem—but regular, daily, negative habits are. There are consequences from allowing things into our lives on a consistent basis. There are some things we all do every day that we may need to stop doing. Then there are some things we don't do every day that we may want to start doing. There are a host of highly productive habits we can incorporate into our lives daily.

I am familiar with a prolific writer who disciplines himself to write at least 30 minutes a day. He is later able to compile all that content into book after book. This is encouraging to me. Even a habit of 15 minutes a day can produce fruit; anyone can find 15 minutes a day for self-improvement. We see in Scripture that God rewards the faithful: *"His master said to him, 'Well done, good and faithful servant. You have been faithful over a little; I will set you over much. Enter into the joy of your master'"* (Matthew 25:21, ESV).

Declaration

Today I will begin to sow seeds that I want to reap. I want to hear the Lord say, "You have been faithful."

Activation

In regard to your purpose, are there some things in your life that you need to stop doing or to start doing?

Ask the Lord about specifics related to your purpose and write down two things you feel would be productive to begin doing in your daily routine.

_____

_____

_____

_____

_____

_____

_____

_____

_____

_____

_____

_____

_____

_____

_____

_____

DAY 41

God Is in Control

Finally, brothers, whatever is true, whatever is honorable,
whatever is just, whatever is pure, whatever is lovely, whatever is
commendable, if there is any excellence, if there is anything worthy
of praise, think about these things. What you have learned and
received and heard and seen in me—practice these things, and
the God of peace will be with you (Philippians 4:8-9, ESV).

A key to living your life of purpose is maintaining a positive attitude by listening to, reading, and paying attention to things that are positive around you. You may ask how that's possible when there is so much negativity surrounding us. The key is learning to look at things through the lens of God's Word. You can even look at challenges you face daily, believing that God is in control and has the best life planned for you. When you look at things with a positive mental attitude, it gives you an incredible edge, and you are a much happier person.

During my life, I have endured betrayal, lies to and about me, theft, slander, false accusation, disappointment, and sorrow. Although these were sad moments, I've still had much more joy than sorrow! Often, it made people angrier that I remained positive; a positive mental attitude is what got me through those situations without offense, bitterness, or anger. I had a boss tell me one time, "Karen, you are stronger than ten acres of garlic!" I took that as a compliment. What made me appear so strong? A positive mental attitude and believing that the Word is true (Romans 8:28).

Declaration

I will think about things that are true, pure, lovely, and excellent. I will look at things through the lens of God's Word and let positivity spill out of me.

Activation

How have you experienced negativity in and around you that affected the outcome of a situation? How has keeping a positive attitude affected your ability to walk out your purpose?

You cannot control what other people do, but you can control how you respond. List some ways you can respond positively to a possibly negative situation in your life.

_____

_____

_____

_____

_____

_____

_____

_____

_____

_____

_____

_____

DAY 42

Excellence Requires Extra Time and Effort

Whatever you do, work heartily, as for the Lord and not for men,
knowing that from the Lord you will receive the inheritance as your
reward. You are serving the Lord Christ (Colossians 3:23-24, ESV).

To fulfill your purpose, be prepared to pay the full price for excellence and count the cost. I must work at this one rather consistently because I like getting things done and done quickly. Excellence usually requires extra time and effort, but the result is worth it in every area. Good examples of this are proofing what you write before you send it, pausing and not rushing an emotional response, and checking grammar when documenting a written process. All these can help assure you're going to develop the best opportunity for excellence. You can utilize these tools, but you don't have to accomplish all of them yourself. By being aware of them, you can surround yourself with a team or put processes in place to help leverage these principles. In the areas where you're not as strong, find a coworker or friend who is. I like to surround myself with people who love details, as this is not an area of strength for me.

Long term, you'll always be happier in your purpose doing things with excellence. Pull the gifts and talents from those in your family, your friends, and your colleagues at work. Hire people who can fill gaps for you. The spirit of excellence is something that pleases God because it reflects His Spirit.

Declaration

I will work heartily for the Lord and develop a spirit of excellence in my life. I will look for others around me who do things with excellence and learn from them.

Activation

How have you made a personal commitment to excellence? If you haven't, why haven't you? In what ways does your work environment value or not value excellence?

List the people and the projects you think about when you hear the word "excellence." Ask the Lord if there are areas in your life that need a spirit of excellence.

_____

_____

_____

_____

_____

_____

_____

_____

_____

_____

_____

_____

_____

_____

_____

DAY 43

Struggle Develops Character

And not only this, but [with joy] let us exult in our sufferings
and rejoice in our hardships, knowing that hardship (distress,
pressure, trouble) produces patient endurance; and endurance,
proven character (spiritual maturity); and proven character,
hope and confident assurance [of eternal salvation]. Such hope
[in God's promises] never disappoints us, because God's love
has been abundantly poured out within our hearts through
the Holy Spirit who was given to us (Romans 5:3-5, AMP).

As you walk out your purpose, you will have ample time to develop persistence and perseverance. These qualities come through enduring difficulties and failures because struggle develops character. Dealing with challenges is cumulative.

The book of James explains that perseverance leads to true faith that helps control our tongue, submit to God's will, have patience, and more. The Holy Spirit's goal is for followers of Jesus to be wise and authentic. You acquire those attributes as you personally build perseverance through trial and error. When you have developed endurance like an athlete, you can tap into your experience, trust God explicitly, hold on to peace, and receive hope that God will see you through every situation.

As you move toward your purpose, you'll face opposition. If Jesus' disciples had not encountered challenges along the way, it would have been much more difficult for them after Jesus ascended into Heaven. The path to obtaining hope includes tribulations, knowing that tribulation produces perseverance; and perseverance, character; and then character, hope. As things come against you, surprise you, or disappoint you, hope based on past tribulations and difficulties catapults you into handling what's ahead so you can push through in a positive way.

Nothing works like God's Word when going through difficulties. God doesn't give us trials and hardships. We all make decisions, not knowing what is ahead. It is encouraging to know that even in our mistakes, God is with us and will help us through all areas of life.

Declaration

God has designed all things to work for my good. I will look at my difficulties as opportunities for the Lord to develop perseverance in me.

Activation

In what ways have you allowed your struggles and difficulties to develop perseverance in your life?

Journal about a hardship that resulted in persistence and endurance. Were you open to the process, or did you have to learn the hard way?

_____

_____

_____

_____

_____

_____

_____

_____

_____

_____

_____

_____

_____

_____

_____

_____

The Power of a Good Mentor

And what you have heard from me in the presence of
many witnesses entrust to faithful men, who will be
able to teach others also (2 Timothy 2:2, ESV).

Older women likewise are to be reverent in behavior,
not slanderers or slaves to much wine. They are to teach
what is good, and so train the young women to love
their husbands and children (Titus 2:3-4, ESV).

God has blessed me throughout my career with
some amazing mentors. Being in relationship
with someone who has experience related to your
purpose can be a game changer. The couple who mentored me encouraged me at every turn, provided speaking
opportunities at events, and genuinely cared about me as a
person. Through their mentorship, I learned about starting a successful business, how to build wealth, and how to
trust God through relationship challenges. I can honestly
say their mentorship has increased the quality of life in my
career, family, and marriage. That is the power of a good
mentor.

Mentorship comes in various forms from purely obser-
vational, quite casual, or very formal. You can be mentored

by your favorite speaker through observing, critiquing, and imitating. Also, you can be mentored by an admired colleague through observing, questioning, and shadowing. Or you can ask someone who is successful in your field to formally mentor you. This may include regular meeting times, sharing of ideas and strategies, and much more, based on mutual agreements and boundaries. You could choose one or more types of mentoring, but I highly recommend having a mentor related to your purpose. Mentorship is a valuable tool found in Scripture and utilized in many professions.

Declaration

Today I will learn from those wiser and more experienced than me. I will gain all the wisdom and knowledge I can from people God has placed around me.

Activation

Describe a time when you have received mentorship or given it. If you have never received mentoring, why not? Is this something you are open to?

List public figures whom you admire, and schedule time to observe them. Ask the Lord who would be a good mentor for you.

_____

_____

_____

_____

_____

_____

_____

_____

_____

_____

_____

_____

_____

_____

Speak Truth and Wisdom in Any Given Moment

The good person out of the good treasure of his heart
produces good, and the evil person out of his evil
treasure produces evil, for out of the abundance of
the heart his mouth speaks (Luke 6:45, ESV).

While walking out your purpose, you could be called at any time to articulate and communicate effectively. Jesus had ready answers for true seekers, as well as hostile opponents. He set the precedent for His followers. You need to be ready to speak truth and wisdom in any given moment. Matthew 22:15-22 describes a scene when the Pharisees intended to trap Jesus, but He turned it around with a ready answer full of wisdom. And Paul, one of the great champions of the faith, mastered the art of persuasion; he was always ready to debate, articulate, defend, and communicate effectively to lead people to truth.

It isn't wise to talk or give a speech about something you don't know or haven't experienced personally. I've learned throughout the years to position myself in areas where I'm experienced. If I do a job, consult, or teach, I develop my knowledge and ability in those areas to a level where, even if I don't have the exact answers, I know enough about the subject to converse intelligently and know where I can find more details if needed.

If you're prepared to be an effective communicator on the spot, you will have an edge wherever you are and in whatever phase of your purpose you find yourself in. Fill your heart with God's Word so it effortlessly overflows from your speech and become masterful in your trade. You will be well equipped with a ready answer.

Declaration

Out of the abundance of my heart I will speak words of kindness and encouragement today. I am well equipped to stand before my peers.

Activation

How well are you typically prepared when asked to give a report or speak on a topic?

Write down some ideas on how you can be better prepared when you are asked to speak. Ask the Lord for some strategies.

_____

_____

_____

_____

_____

_____

_____

_____

_____

_____

_____

_____

_____

_____

_____

_____

God Gave Us Our Emotions

A soft answer turns away wrath, but a harsh word stirs up anger. The
tongue of the wise uses knowledge rightly, but the mouth of fools
pours forth foolishness. The eyes of the Lord are in every place,
keeping watch on the evil and the good. A gentle tongue is a tree of
life, but perverseness in it breaks the spirit (Proverbs 15:1-4, NKJV).

L iving out your purpose will not always be smooth
sailing. There will be days that are loaded with anger
and sadness as well as joy and delight. Your emotions
are not good or bad. They are there to tell you something is
happening at a heart level. But don't let emotions rule your
life, decision making, or relationships. God has given us
emotions, so you know there's a positive side to them. After
all, happy is an emotion! And sometimes when you have
emotions of anger or hurt, they are clues that you need to
pay attention to and grab hold of the underlying root of
those feelings. The apostle Paul said to be angry but don't
sin (Ephesians 4:26). When you learn to handle negative
emotions, your life becomes more peaceful.

In emotional situations, it helps to back up, soften your
language, pause, and then ask, "What is the worst thing that
can happen in this circumstance?" Emotions can cause you
to see things much bigger, worse, or more impactful than

they really are. When you learn to control your emotions, it helps you understand why you're feeling the way you are. If you're to become eligible for more responsibility, a larger sphere of influence, or more authority, one requirement is to keep your emotions intact. Unhealthy emotions can cause issues, but healthy emotions are a joy and make tasks easier to handle.

Declaration

My emotions will not control me. I will submit my feelings to the Lord and ask for wisdom in understanding and dealing with them.

Activation

Think of a situation where you let your emotions run away. What were the effects of out-of-control emotions?

Think of a time when you thought, *I wish I hadn't said that.* Write down what you could have changed. Ask the Lord what you could have changed.

_____

_____

_____

_____

_____

_____

_____

_____

_____

_____

_____

_____

_____

_____

_____

_____

DAY 47

Criticism Can Be Positive or Negative

If you listen to constructive criticism, you will be at home among the wise. If you reject discipline, you only harm yourself; but if you listen to correction, you grow in understanding. Fear of the Lord teaches wisdom; humility precedes honor (Proverbs 15:31-33, NLT).

C riticism will always be part of the process in walking out your purpose but it has no authority over you except what you give it. It is not enjoyable having other people tell us what we're doing wrong. But to be successful, lead a business, grow your sphere of influence, manage employees, or even manage your household, it's important to learn how to handle criticism. There are two kinds of criticism—positive and negative. You must recognize which type of criticism is being directed at you and handle it appropriately.

To receive positive criticism, you need to trust the person giving the feedback. Knowing the heart of the person, along with his or her character and value shown for you, can help prepare you for feedback, allowing you to hear the criticism or suggestion as positive, not negative. You and I are not required to listen to or heed negative criticism. If you're being criticized outside the boundaries of your well-being, just let it go. When a person is carelessly saying something to hurt me, I have no obligation to consider it. Know the difference between the two types of criticism. Accept the positive and set aside the negative.

Declaration

I will listen to constructive criticism and will not reject feedback. Open my eyes, Lord, to discern the difference between positive and negative feedback.

Activation

In this day of social media, people are quick to criticize and slow to consider consequences. Do you find yourself being critical on social media? In what ways can you avoid being critical?

Journal about a time you received positive criticism and how you felt. Now journal about a time you received negative criticism. Compare your feelings.

_____

_____

_____

_____

_____

_____

_____

_____

_____

_____

_____

_____

_____

Problems Are Opportunities for Success

> They will not live in fear or dread of what may come, for their
> hearts are firm, ever secure in their faith. Steady and strong,
> they will not be afraid, but will calmly face their every foe
> until they all go down in defeat (Psalm 112:7-8, TPT).

Working out of your purpose brings confidence and freedom from fear. Problems are opportunities for success. I know that seems cliché, but it really is a way for you to exercise your faith in God. When problems arise, instead of worrying or stressing, you can be disciplined to give the situation to the Lord. Find Scriptures that minister to you in that area, and release your worries to Him. He can move in grace to solve issues and resolve problems.

In avoiding stress and worry, ask, *Is this what I'm called to do? Is this my purpose, or have I wandered into something God never asked me to do?* Then make the necessary adjustments. Another key is to be thankful. When you express thanksgiving in the midst of trouble, you can know that God is going to bring peace. The Word of God is a weapon for us to use. When stress, fear, and worry come, you can stand strong on the Word of God, seeing things through that lens. There is no need for you to suffer from worry or stress. Just remember that if God has promised it, He will perform it on your behalf.

Declaration

Lord, I am releasing my stress to You, and I'm trusting You to bring about the results promised in Your Word. I thank You and honor You for it. I'm moving forward in my purpose stress-free.

Activation

What are the current stressors or worries in your life?

Write down the things that are stressing you right now. Beside each one, leave a space for the Lord to speak peace to you about it.

_____

_____

_____

_____

_____

_____

_____

_____

_____

_____

_____

_____

_____

_____

_____

_____

Decisiveness Instills Confidence

> If any of you lacks wisdom, let him ask of God, who gives to all liberally and without reproach, and it will be given to him. But let him ask in faith, with no doubting, for he who doubts is like a wave of the sea driven and tossed by the wind. For let not that man suppose that he will receive anything from the Lord; he is a double-minded man, unstable in all his ways (James 1:5-8, NKJV).

Indecisive leadership is discouraging and can hijack your purpose. James 1:5-8 tells us that a wavering or double-minded person will receive nothing from the Lord. Double-minded people move from one opinion to another, eventually incapacitating their faith and resulting in inconsistent choices. The Old Testament describes the wavering mentality of Israel's believing and not believing. Their entry into the Promised Land was delayed 40 years because of disbelief. There are times when you might have a little doubt, but when you're decisive, you can trust the Lord with your decision. If I start wavering, it is because I'm trusting in my abilities to accomplish something on my own rather than in His abilities. God did not say He would only bless you if you never made mistakes. He said He would bless you. Period.

Being decisive is encouraging and instills confidence in you and those around you. This is never truer than in your home. If a decision needs to be made concerning a family issue, the people involved are waiting for decisiveness to show up. Your teenagers need to hear a yes or no (though they are hoping for a yes), not a maybe or ask me tomorrow. If you seek God in your decisions and do the best you can, His grace is sufficient. He causes all things to work together for good. In leadership and in life, He can steer a ship in motion. Your decisiveness will cause those you influence to be successful.

Declaration

I will not be like the sea tossed and driven by the wind. I will seek the Lord before I make decisions and walk boldly where He directs me.

Activation

Describe a time when you made a decision, and then wondered, *Am I right? Am I wrong? Maybe I should have done something different.*

Journal about your decisions for one day. Mark the ones that were decisive and those that were wavering. Ask the Lord how to turn them all into decisive decisions.

_____

_____

_____

_____

_____

_____

_____

_____

_____

_____

_____

_____

_____

_____

DAY 50

Being Purposeful

For it is [not your strength, but it is] God who is effectively at
work in you, both to will and to work [that is, strengthening,
energizing, and creating in you the longing and the ability to fulfill
your purpose] for His good pleasure (Philippians 2:13 AMP).

When Dave and I got married, we took time to talk about and document our vision as a couple for the upcoming year. We discussed our priorities, things we wanted to accomplish, and goals we wanted to attain. Two items from the list of things that we agreed were important to us as a couple were staying fit and praying together. We knew that if we just listed our goals without making a realistic, actionable plan to accomplish them in our everyday lives, the year would pass, and we would still be where we started.

We designed and committed to a daily schedule of exercise each morning—taking a walk together one day and doing a form of Pilates the next. Then, on Pilates day, we chose a Scripture from Grandma Esther's prayer box, talked about it, and prayed together based on that Scripture at the end of our workout. Even when we travel, we follow this schedule. At this point, it's a way of life. We have attained our goal of staying fit and praying together by being purposeful in how we start our day. God is at work in us to fulfill our purpose for His good pleasure. We just need to work His plan.

Declaration

God is at work, strengthening and energizing me for His good pleasure. I am destined for success.

Activation

What goals are you struggling to achieve? What are some reasons that you are not achieving them?

Write down one goal you have on your heart. Ask the Lord to give you some doable steps to begin rolling toward that goal.

_____

_____

_____

_____

_____

_____

_____

_____

_____

_____

_____

_____

_____

_____

_____

_____

DAY 51

Count the Cost on the Front End

I glorified you on earth, having accomplished the work
that you gave me to do. And now, Father, glorify me in
your own presence with the glory that I had with you
before the world existed (John 17:4-5, ESV).

So when Jesus had received the sour wine, He said, "It is finished!"
And bowing His head, He gave up His spirit (John 19:30, NKJV).

B e a finisher in your life and in the pursuit of your
purpose. Ideas without actions will not yield results;
but if you don't quit, you win. You are created to
bring projects and situations to the finish line. Jesus is the
best example for us of a Finisher. Without the work Jesus
did, we would be lost. Without all the suffering He went
through, all the words He spoke, all the prayers He prayed,
all the wisdom He poured into the disciples, God's plan
would not have been fulfilled. Jesus showed us the value of
a completed work, which is to glorify God.

To fulfill your purpose, it is important to develop a
process to help you finish what you've started. A process
requires wisdom, knowledge, and thinking strategically on
the front end. It requires asking questions such as: Do you
have enough money to complete the project? Do you have

enough personal bandwidth? Do you need more team members? What will the finished project look like? In all your endeavors, the goal is to stand with Paul and be able to say, *"I have fought the good fight, I have finished the race, I have kept the faith"* (2 Timothy 4:7, ESV).

Declaration

By the grace of God, I will finish what God has given me to do to fulfill my purpose. I will count the cost and walk boldly through my next project to the finish.

Activation

Are you great at starting, but not so great at finishing? Where do you think that tendency comes from?

Journal about a project that came to a good finish. Analyze what you did and why. Ask the Lord what He sees.

_____

_____

_____

_____

_____

_____

_____

_____

_____

_____

_____

_____

_____

_____

_____

_____

DAY 52

You Have Favor
with God and People

A good man obtains favor from the Lord, but a man of wicked
intentions He will condemn (Proverbs 12:2, NKJV).

You are an ambassador, giving people their first glimpse of Jesus. Take time to be favorable in appearance (dress and countenance), giving authenticity to what you carry. Expect the best because God has provided for the fulfillment of your purpose. His Word says that He has given us favor in the sight of God and humans. The understanding that God has provided favor helps you confidently approach a situation that you feel nervous about. If you go into the situation with your mind set on the truth that God has already given you favor, you can relax, agree with His Word, and approach situations expecting the best.

This applies to every area of your life. All these principles for success have a spiritual context based on the Word of God. There is a relational context, a work context, and a financial context. When my expectation is favor in a situation, I can take it and lean into God for the results. This is such a stress-free way to live.

Do you look like you are carrying the love of Jesus? Do you look like you are prosperous in your business? Do you look like you are full of joy and full of peace? Doing so will help you bring the favor of God into conversations and situations to create an atmosphere that reflects His goodness and grace.

Declaration

God has provided for me, so I will expect the best in every situation. I have the full favor of the Lord.

Activation

Have you ever walked into a room full of people and started thinking, *What if they don't like me?* How can you change your self-talk to make you more confident of your calling and purpose?

Keep track of your self-talk for one day. Mark the thoughts that reflect God's favor and those that reflect doubt. Talk to the Lord about it.

_____

_____

_____

_____

_____

_____

_____

_____

_____

_____

_____

_____

_____

_____

God Rewards a Good Steward

There is precious treasure and oil in the house of the wise [who prepare for the future], but a short-sighted and foolish man [person] swallows it up and wastes it (Proverbs 21:20, AMP).

I t is wise throughout your life of purpose to keep financial reserves available for emergencies. Having a cushion to help weather bumps in the road is good stewardship. God has called us to be good stewards, and many Scriptures outline how to manage our finances. Good stewardship helps us manage money, time, and resources, affecting every area of our life. When combined with His promises in Deuteronomy 8:18, we can learn a lot about finances from a spiritual perspective. God wants you and me to be well taken care of with our finances, along with having enough to establish His Kingdom.

From a natural perspective, what happens when we're not good stewards? Have you ever been in debt or had a large credit card balance, and all at once you realize how much interest you are paying each month? Have you outspent the amount of money you make? Let me tell you, it is not a good place to be. The number one cause of failed marriages is money issues. When we don't have the money to pay our bills, put food on the table, or buy the things we know we need to take care of our family, it is very stressful. When at all possible, have financial reserves to remove this stressor from your life and relationships. God rewards a good steward.

Declaration

I will not be short-sighted, foolish, and wasteful. I will be wise and prepare for the future. I will receive the reward of a good steward.

Activation

How familiar are you with the principles of biblical stewardship? How effective have you been applying these concepts to your life?

Look up in the Bible all the Scriptures on stewardship you can find. Begin to dig deeper into how those Scriptures can affect your financial life. Journal your results.

_____

_____

_____

_____

_____

_____

_____

_____

_____

_____

_____

_____

_____

_____

DAY 54

Be a Lifelong Learner

Before disaster the heart of a man is haughty and filled
with self-importance, but humility comes before honor.
He who answers before he hears [the facts]—it is folly
and shame to him (Proverbs 18:12-13 AMP).

When living in your purpose, it is very valuable to ask questions. Be a lifelong learner, and surround yourself with people who are smarter than you. To be a good leader, you need people on your team who know more about their particular subject than you do. Asking questions such as, "What do you think? What are your thoughts about this? What do you think is best?" is an excellent way to end a conversation or email.

Jesus was a master of asking questions. As a matter of fact, when you spend time with Him, He asks lots of questions: "What are you thinking here? How could you have responded differently? What does My Word say?" He helps me know what I'm thinking when I'm not sure. If you seek to understand, you can move forward and be a positive, proactive influence in whatever it is you are called to do. It's important to be willing to hear opinions that don't match your own. Sometimes as a leader, that can be difficult because we think we need to be right. When you allow people to offer input and then ask them questions, you open up an opportunity to teach and expand their knowledge as well as yours. Humility comes before honor. Humble yourself and ask questions.

Declaration

I will not answer before I hear the facts, and I will humbly ask for wisdom and guidance from those around me.

Activation

How good are you at asking questions and seeking feedback from your team, colleagues, or family? How can you improve in this area?

List the number of times you ask questions in one day. Are there a lot or only a few? Ask the Lord how to become a learner.

_____

_____

_____

_____

_____

_____

_____

_____

_____

_____

_____

_____

_____

_____

DAY 55

You Decide for You

For all the promises of God find their Yes in him. That
is why it is through him that we utter our Amen to
God for his glory (2 Corinthians 1:20, ESV).

You have the power of choice. When you discover your purpose and begin walking it out, you will be confronted with choices every day. Not only choices for major decisions, but choices for what to believe and who you want to become. No one but you can stop you from being successful. Don't allow roadblocks or discouragement to have more power in your life than God's Word. You are in charge of you.

The key to this is finding your identity in Jesus and who He says you are. Now, this doesn't mean you won't have challenges or ever be treated unfairly. But it does mean that if you see challenges through the lens of being a victor not a victim, you can walk through any situation to the other side and see success.

I encourage you when looking at your life to realize you have the power of choice. When I am tempted to say that I can't do this or that because of someone else, I know that's not the truth. Because, when it comes down to it, I am in charge of me, and you are in charge of you. One of the most important keys to success is to remember that you and I have the power of choice—and we can choose success.

Declaration

I will shout "Yes and Amen" to the promises of God. I am in charge of me, and I will walk in the ways of the Lord.

Activation

Describe a time when you believed you were a victim and someone else was to blame for your struggles. How has your perspective changed looking back on that situation? How can you keep yourself from having a victim mentality?

Journal your thoughts on a victim mentality. Ask the Lord if you are dealing with a victim mentality and how you can change that to a victor mentality.

_____

_____

_____

_____

_____

_____

_____

_____

_____

_____

_____

_____

_____

_____

Despite Failures, You Are Loved and Accepted by God

For the lovers of God may suffer adversity and stumble seven times, but they will continue to rise over and over again. But the unrighteous are brought down by just one calamity and will never be able to rise again (Proverbs 24:16, TPT).

I've come to realize that every opportunity toward purpose that I'm presented with also has the risk of failure. Our heavenly Father doesn't protect us from risk automatically, because that would hinder us from the opportunity to be successful. He understands that we will make mistakes as we learn to walk in belief and trust, and that mistakes bring about growth. Despite failures, you are still loved and accepted by God. Hebrews 10:38 encourages us not to pull back or shrink in fear. And Ephesians 1:6 says that we are made accepted in Jesus. You can rest assured that His love for you doesn't change with your successes or failures.

Proverbs 24:16 gives us the definition of success and failure. Success is persistence to accomplish a desired outcome, no matter how long it takes. And failure is quitting before the desired outcome is reached. God's Word doesn't say that you do not fall. He looks on your heart; and when you persist in believing and acting upon His Word, you build on His sure foundation. In Hebrews, the writer says that Abraham was counted as righteous because he believed, even though at one point he quit holding on to God's promise (Genesis 16). Keep in mind on your way to becoming successful, you will likely experience some failures—but don't quit or give up!

Declaration

By the grace of God, I will rise over and over again. My mistakes will not be my downfall, but will be steps into wisdom and growth.

Activation

How do you view failure: as ultimate defeat or as a stepping-stone to success? Why?

Journal through your thoughts on success and failure. Ask the Lord to show you how He sees success and failure.

_____

_____

_____

_____

_____

_____

_____

_____

_____

_____

_____

_____

_____

_____

_____

Weathering the Seasons of Life

There is a season (a time appointed) for everything
and a time for every delight and event or purpose
under heaven (Ecclesiastes 3:1, AMP).

There will be times when success will look different
depending on your time and season of life. For
example, in my twenties, with my first job out of
college, I was just happy to have a job where I could pay
rent and buy a car without help from my dad. Success for
me was moving into a position where I had some auton-
omy and responsibility. Twenty years later, that would not
have looked like success to me. I was in a totally different
season of purpose.

Then there was the season my son Levi was born. It
was important for me to be a good mom, so an executive
travel schedule wouldn't have looked like success when my
primary responsibility was raising my son. Seasons change
periodically, and it can be confusing. But first things first.
You need to have the Word of God as a foundation in your
life.

As you strive to follow the Word and fulfill your purpose, you'll be able to grab hold of the Lord for strength.

You'll grow through the comfort of the Holy Spirit, through Bible teachings, through sharing stories, and through learning from others' experiences. There are people currently in positions where you could conceivably be in two or three years. Ask questions and learn how they got there. But above all, know that the foundation is the Word of God.

Declaration

Whatever my season may be, I will trust the Lord's timing in my life. Father, make me ready for any transition You have for me today.

Activation

What season are you in? Are you in a season that's ending? Are you in a season that should've ended, but you're just hanging on because of the comfort level there?

If you are beginning to feel a stirring inside toward a transition, list the items of "holy discontent," and allow the Lord to nudge you to the next level.

_____

_____

_____

_____

_____

_____

_____

_____

_____

_____

_____

_____

_____

_____

DAY 58

God Gives Wisdom Generously

If any of you lacks wisdom [to guide him through a decision or circumstance], he is to ask of [our benevolent] God, who gives to everyone generously and without rebuke or blame, and it will be given to him (James 1:5, AMP).

When God gives you a big assignment, you're going to have to work to gain knowledge and skills to carry it out. This applies at home, in your family, and in your work or business and in fulfilling your purpose. Sometimes you can gain knowledge in a supernatural way, where God gives you a hidden talent. Through being obedient in accepting the assignment, that new talent begins to show, and you end up with wisdom and abilities you didn't know you had. You'll receive knowledge that you didn't receive education or training to achieve. People around you may begin to ask, "How did you see this? How do you know to do this?" And you realize that your ability isn't something everyone has—it is from God.

Other times, you can ask God for wisdom, and He grants it either through His Word or His Spirit. Then there are times when you grow in knowledge through good old-fashioned study and hard work. In business for instance, you need to learn how much you should charge, what your costs will be, whom you should hire, and so forth. You need to develop this type of practical knowledge to be successful in your purpose, whether it is business, ministry, or home. Educate yourself to become a master in your field, whatever it is God has given you. His wisdom and knowledge are valuable in every area of your purposeful life.

Declaration

God has wisdom available for me in generous, overflowing amounts. I will commit myself to learning and growing wiser in my purpose.

Activation

In what areas of your life are you currently lacking wisdom? Are you spending your energy trudging toward an answer, or are you asking the Lord for solutions?

Journal about a time you realized something about you was not common to everyone—it is special about you. Ask the Lord for more gifts and talents to help you walk in your purpose.

_____

_____

_____

_____

_____

_____

_____

_____

_____

_____

_____

_____

_____

Your Character Affects Your Purpose

But you shall remember [with profound respect] the Lord your God, for it is He who is giving you power to make wealth, that He may confirm His covenant which He swore (solemnly promised) to your fathers, as it is this day (Deuteronomy 8:18, AMP).

Your character is linked to your economic capacity and is an area in which you need continual growth. Character is one of those things the Lord works in you, and it is important in economic capacity. Does your character make you safe for money and wealth? Money itself doesn't have power—it amplifies what's in your heart. What you do with money brings power and influence in the natural. It's a reflection and underlines what's inside you. Your character helps determine your economic capacity to be able to handle wealth. And the more you're able to handle wealth from a character perspective, the more you can be entrusted with riches to expand God's Kingdom.

Today's verse in Deuteronomy 8:18 contains a relational blessing. God is the giver. He is our Power Source that flows from a relationship with Him. Power is the strength, force, means, substance, and capacity—whether physical, mental, or spiritual—necessary to obtain wealth. This wealth includes resources, riches, substance, and influence. God gives us this power to confirm His covenant. Material blessings are included in the promises to the patriarchs and to you and me as their descendants and as joint heirs in Christ. God empowers you to create wealth to demonstrate His covenant—and influence is key to expanding His Kingdom and fulfilling your purpose.

Declaration

Lord, You are the One who gives me the power to make wealth, and I receive Your blessing. I will walk in integrity, making myself safe for everything You have for me.

Activation

In what ways are you a safe place for money? In what ways are you not? What aspects of your financial life may need to be adjusted by God's Word?

Journal through your thoughts on character and integrity. Ask the Lord to show you His plan for your character.

_____

_____

_____

_____

_____

_____

_____

_____

_____

_____

_____

_____

_____

_____

DAY 60

Your Purpose Makes the Best Use of Your Gifts

Blessed and worthy of praise be the God and Father of our Lord Jesus Christ, who has blessed us with every spiritual blessing in the heavenly realms in Christ, just as [in His love] He chose us in Christ [actually selected us for Himself as His own] before the foundation of the world, so that we would be holy [that is, consecrated, set apart for Him, purpose-driven] and blameless in His sight. In love He predestined and lovingly planned for us to be adopted to Himself as [His own] children through Jesus Christ, in accordance with the kind intention and good pleasure of His will (Ephesians 1:3-5, AMP).

When I discovered my purpose, my life catapulted. All areas of my life took off when I had an understanding of my purpose in the Lord. Anything I considered success in the past paled compared to living out my purpose through Him. Knowing how He designed me—how I approach work—helps me to make the best use of His gifts and talents. It also brings me the most joy and protects me from finding my identity in performance or other people's opinions.

Even within your purpose, any venture you pursue will hit a rough patch at some point. Difficulties help you grow, but God doesn't allow challenges to harm you. Your passion for the Lord will get you through hardships, knowing that He has called you. You can look to Him to bring resolution and to give you strength. Go to the Lord and let Him know your struggle. Trust Him to infuse you with strength and passion and purpose for what He's called you to do.

We all have moments when we don't feel equipped or when we feel like giving up, but we can't be ruled by feelings. Hold on to the passion He's given you toward Him and your purpose.

Declaration

I have been consecrated, set apart, and given a purpose. I will hold on to the passion He's given me for Him and for my purpose.

Activation

In what ways have you allowed your passion to cool after repeated struggles? How are you allowing God to renew your strength and resolution?

List your purpose and your gifts and talents. List the difficulties you are having in a particular area. Ask the Lord to show you where these two lists meet and what His available solutions are.

_____

_____

_____

_____

_____

_____

_____

_____

_____

_____

_____

_____

_____

_____

Conclusion

And the Lord answered me: "Write the vision; make it plain on tablets, so he may run who reads it" (Habakkuk 2:2, ESV).

What is your purpose? Write it down.

God gave the prophet Habakkuk a helpful directive, *"And the Lord answered me: 'Write the vision; make it plain on tablets, so he may run who reads it.'"* It's interesting to note that God gave this instruction to the prophet after listening to Habakkuk complain twice. God is relational and solution oriented; the advice to make the vision plain for communication is beneficial to us.

What is your purpose? Write it down, and you will understand how to live it and communicate it to others. In your purpose and vision statement, include what your purpose looks like for you, your family, your work, and your dreams. God has plans of joy and success for every area of your life.

I hope this devotional has been an encouragement and a catalyst for you. Please use the individual days to periodically refresh your heart on your journey to a life filled with purpose. Whether you have known your purpose for years or you discovered it while walking through this devotional, I pray life and joy and peace over you.

I would love to hear from you. Please email me at info@karenconrad.net with your stories of victory and hope. Also, feel free to ask questions, share suggestions, and for more resources, please visit KarenConrad.net.

May God richly bless all you set your hand to accomplish.

Amen.

About the Author

Karen Conrad applies her purpose in everything she does. Whether starting and building a successful business, creating a beautiful home for your family, or overcoming debilitating fear, Karen helps people step into their destiny. She believes that people are created with a unique purpose by God and helps people from all walks of life find their purpose then brings vision to reality and success.

Karen currently lives in the Dallas-Fort Worth area in Texas with her amazing husband, Dave. They work together in business coaching and ministry, and along with Karen's son, Levi, they have started a real estate venture, Sweet Tea Properties. You can follow along with their remodeling adventures through her Sweet Tea Hospitality Series available for streaming on Liftable.TV or for download at Sweetea.tv.

Karen's teachings are found on Gospel Truth TV, Kingdom Building TV, Eternal Life TV, KBTV, and YouTube. Her book, *The Promise of Purpose: Proven Strategies to Reach Your God-Given Potential,* is available in her online shop or wherever your favorite books are sold.

Contact Information

WEBSITE:
https://www.karenconrad.net/

EMAIL:
info@karenconrad.net

BLOG:
https://www.karenconrad.
net/karen-conrad-blog/

RESOURCES:
https://www.karenconrad.net/shop/

Harrison House Books
by Karen Conrad

The Promise of Purpose:
Proven Strategies to Reach Your God-Given Potential

Equipping Believers to Walk in the Abundant Life

John 10:10b

Connect with us on

Facebook @ HarrisonHousePublishers

and Instagram @ HarrisonHousePublishing

so you can stay up to date with news

about our books and our authors.

Visit us at **www.harrisonhouse.com**